The Restoration of the American Natural Rights Republic:

Correcting the Consequences of the Republican Party Abdication of Natural Rights and Individual Freedom

Laurie Thomas Vass

I0086459

The Great American Business & Economics Press
GABBY Press

The Restoration of the American Natural Rights Republic:
Correcting the Economic Consequences of the Republican Party Abdication
of Natural Rights and Individual Freedom

Table of Contents

Schedule of Diagrams and Charts

Since 2008, callers into the Rush Limbaugh radio program have been expressing a common despair about why the Republicans did not fight to protect individual freedoms from the socialist transformation of America, when the moment of battle with global socialist tyranny arrived.

This book explains why the Republican Party can never be expected to defend individual natural rights. It offers solutions to the consequences of the Republican abdication by outlining the restoration of a natural rights republic that restores the American cultural ethic of the "self-made" citizen.

In Madison's flawed arrangement of checks and balances, the Republicans obtained a privileged position to be one party of a two party system, based upon social class interest of the well born. Madison wanted to restore the British class system of aristocratic government.

Madison's two party class political system has devolved into a dysfunctional global tyranny, where no political party represents the common interest of citizen liberty.

The Democrats have morphed into a global socialist party, and no longer represent the working class.

The Republicans have morphed into a global corporatist party, which no longer defends American sovereignty.

Limbaugh's response to the callers has gone through a transformation, primarily from being a defender of the status quo Republicans, to being more like the arguments of the anti-federalists in 1787.

His words for this criticism are that the Republicans are part of "the political elite in Washington."

An early explanation, before the election of 2012, offered to callers by Limbaugh for the Republican abdication of liberty, is that the Republicans were scared of being called racists, if they opposed Obama.

The caller below is representative of this expression of despair about why the Republicans were failing to fight against the socialists, with Limbaugh's response about racism.

April 26, 2011. BEGIN TRANSCRIPT

CALLER: I want to tell you up front I'm on a cell phone, so we have that out of the way. But I wanted to try to explain why I think that Donald Trump, who I think is just a horrible candidate for the Republicans, is catching on with so many Republicans. It's because he talks like he's got some balls. And I'm begging, I'm begging for somebody in the Republican Party to step forward that's got some balls. You know what I'm saying?

RUSH: I do think he has a skewed view of conservatism. I do. I think somebody's given him a bit of a misread on the conservative base. So I'll grant you that. But it is a problem. Look, I'm not being serious. I was joking. I know what you mean when you say people lack some fortitude. I don't know what the fear is. I mean I've tried to figure it out. I've considered still a fear of race, any criticism of Obama is gonna result in being called racist. That fear I think is always gonna be there. I think fear of the Republican hierarchy. There is this notion that you wait 'til it's your turn.

Over a period of several years, Limbaugh's explanation of the Republican behavior began to change to incorporate a type of political symbiosis between the Republicans and the Democrats.

He began to explain that all special interests tended to form a coalition in Washington, that he calls the "political elite."

June 14, 2013. BEGIN TRANSCRIPT.

RUSH: Kansas City. Betty, hi. Welcome to the EIB Network. Great to have you here. Hello.

CALLER: Hi, Rush. I was reading the website, and I think that someone said this yesterday, but I was driving down the road, and you were saying we're just missing something on the amnesty bill, why in the world would Republicans support something that will cause their party to lose in the future. And I was just thinking, well, they'll just become the Democrats -- now, I'm probably being reactionary, but I'm thinking, they'll probably just become the Democrats that they are already are. I am so disappointed in my party. I expect to disagree with the Democrat Party. But I disagree with my party. I'm a Republican, or at least I thought I was.

RUSH: The bottom line is that the Republican Party is embarrassed by its own base. The Republican Party is ashamed of its base. They accept the Democrat caricature of the Republican base. Southern, hayseed hicks, pro-lifers, pickup-truck-driving, gun-rack-in-the-back-window people, chewing tobacco and going to church and talking about God all the time.

But they really see 'em as a bunch of zealots when it comes to abortion. And all these guys I'm talking about have wives who nag 'em about it, don't want any part of the pro-life crowd, embarrassed to be with them at the conventions. So the theory goes that this is a way to get rid of the Republican base. Supporting amnesty and having the Democrats win big-time elections after this is a way for the party to finally get rid of its base. Now, you say, "Well, replace it with what?"

In the most recent period, Limbaugh has sharpened his analysis of Republican Party to include an explanation of why Republicans cooperate with Democrats, when cooperation could possibly result in the death of the Republican Party.

January 14, 2014. BEGIN TRANSCRIPT.

RUSH: Look at every issue that comes up. They give the Democrats all or a part of what they want trying to buy peace and love and affection, and it just never works. So extending unemployment benefits... Here's Obama's economic policy: Extending federal unemployment benefits, raising the federal minimum wage, and amnesty. That's Obama's big economic push. That's what we're told is going to be his focus in the State of the Union show.

January 24, 2014. BEGIN TRANSCRIPT.

RUSH: So, I mean, the upshot here is that you take a look at any national poll, immigration reform, amnesty, it's nowhere near the top when people are asked to name the most important issues they think are facing the country. No reason to do this. And yet the Republican leadership is as desirous and as action oriented, if not more so, than the Democrat majority is in pushing for amnesty. Yet it's the law of the land. But the House Republican leadership wants to go for it.

Now, we know why. Chamber of Commerce and moneyed donors. Donors to mainstream Republicans are saying they want amnesty, they need the new cheap labor, they can't keep going like this. They need it and they'll do anything they can to get it. If it takes amnesty, fine. They don't care about the cultural impact or the rest of it; they just need the labor. And these people depend on these donors for reelection, and so that explains it. Yet it's the law of the land.

By 2014, Limbaugh was becoming increasingly skeptical about the principles that guided the Republican Party.

January 31, 2014. BEGIN TRANSCRIPT.

RUSH: Now, let me close the loop on immigration. We sit here, it doesn't make any sense. It's the end of the Republican Party. The polling data all shows it. The people that would be granted amnesty are not gonna vote Republican because of this or anything else. I mean, not without a lot of work. And the Republican Party being so publicly for amnesty is not going to change how these people vote. I don't know if the Republicans think that's going to happen. I do know that the prevailing thought or theory is really baked in total defensiveness.

Why are the Republicans willing to commit suicide? Because that's what it is. The fact is we haven't seen the Republican Party act much like the opposition party yet. Whenever some individual Republicans do pop up in opposition, they get cut down by other Republicans. I'm gonna tell you, folks, sometimes I end up angrier at Republicans and what they're saying than I get at Democrats these days.

Limbaugh's most recent explanations are getting closer to the truth about the Republican Party. In this most recent incarnation, under Madison's rules of procedure, the Republicans are the party of corporate globalism.

The Republicans need to be seen as representing a special interest group, operating within the framework of the checks and balances of social classes, created by Madison and the Founding Federalists.

It is a mistake for the callers to Rush Limbaugh's program to believe that the Republicans were anything other than the incarnation of the natural aristocracy, under Madison's flawed system of checks and balances. Those callers just assumed that the U. S. Constitution had safeguards that would protect freedom when the battle with socialist tyranny arrived.

They have discovered that the Republicans have abdicated their historic responsibility to defend constitutional natural rights, because Madison's arrangement did not require that of the Republicans.

For Republicans, a "more perfect union" means promoting a single special interest of corporate globalism, protected and enhanced by the Federal government.

For Republicans, corporate globalism, and the defense of natural rights, do not connect.

The Republicans do not see themselves as the opposition party to the socialists because the socialist agenda of global socialism is not detrimental to the Republican end game of advocating global corporatism.

In Madison's 1787 arrangement, one party, the virtuous elites, advocated the financial interests of the elites. The other party, representing the non-elites, could vote every four years to accept or reject the elites who were to rule them.

This book explains one part of the dysfunctional political system in terms of what the Republican abdication of freedom means to American citizen liberty

Madison's idea was to create a U. S. Senate that functioned like the British House of Lords, and have a President that functioned like the British king.

Madison supported the resolution of John Dickson, a federalist delegate from Delaware, on the creation of the Senate. Dickson's resolution stated that, "we ought to carry it through such a refining process as will assimilate it as near as may be to the House of Lords in England."

Madison's logic of restoring the British class system of government in America is that the elites realized that it had been their connection with British royalty, prior to the revolution, that had granted them their privileged status to run their colonies, and to speculate in lands and war bonds.

The natural aristocracy never supported the initial natural rights constitution of 1776, and were intent on overthrowing the natural rights republic, as soon as the opportunity presented itself, in 1787.

Gouverneur Morris, an elite from New York, who helped Madison overthrow the Articles of Confederation, wrote, in 1774, "that the British connection was the guarantee of the existing aristocratic order...after the revolution, they engaged with conservatives in other states in undoing the Articles of Confederation." (The Articles of Confederation, Merrill Jensen).

During the 1787 convention, the Founding Federalists thought that the right term for the Chief Executive was king. The issue of what to call the executive was finally resolved when George Washington said it would be more politically acceptable to the non-elites to call him the President.

In Madison's political party arrangement, the Republican Party, today, has morphed into the party of the rich and the well born, and most importantly, from Madison's perspective, the virtuous. As their ancestors had been in 1775, and 1787, the Republicans today engage in global speculation, and impose disastrous trade policies that serve to undermine the nation's sovereignty.

George Mason correctly identified Madison's ploy about the virtuous as a reincarnation of the British advocacy of "virtual representation."

Madison solved the two great political conflicts of 1785 by insulating the financial interests of the virtuous from the non-virtuous.

In the first political conflict between the farmers who were oppressed by taxes, Madison eliminated the possibility of the states issuing paper money, forcing farmers to pay their taxes in gold or silver.

In the second great conflict between wealthy bondholders and tax payers, Madison established justice for the bondholders by eliminating the possibility that the state assemblies would grant "relief" to the tax payers on the payment of interest to the "virtuous" bondholders.

Madison's new House of Lords acted as a powerful check against the democratic impulses of the farmers. Nine out of ten Americans made their living on farms, but not one of the 51 delegates to the 1787 convention were farmers.

All the delegates of 1787 were selected from the new American aristocracy. All the delegates were land speculators or war bond speculators, with a personal financial interest in skewing the constitutional rules to benefit themselves.

Madison ensured the authority of the central government to enforce his system of justice by inserting the clause, "to insure domestic tranquility" meaning the use of military force to quell the farmer's demands for a different kind of justice.

The rich and the well born were never intended to protect the natural rights enshrined in the Declaration of Independence, because in Madison's scheme, the purpose of the Constitution was to create the civil procedures of a "more perfect union," by placing a disproportionate balance of power in the hands of America's natural aristocracy, precisely because they were virtuous.

According to Madison, the natural aristocracy was comprised of men who had virtue, and this quality of virtue would allow them to make disinterested decisions on behalf of the non-elite.

Madison, and the Federalists, lied to the American public about their intentions to overthrow the Articles of Confederation, because they knew that if they had told the truth about their intent to re-impose the British class system of politics that the states would never have sent representatives.

As it turned out, several states saw through Madison's lie and chose not to send delegates to the convention, and several delegates who did attend, left early and refused to sign the document.

Sometime, around 1790, Madison appeared to regret his mistake in thinking that virtuous aristocracy would promote the common wealth of all citizens. By that time, it was too late. The damage caused by Madison's arrangement was already done.

As William Maclay, a U. S. Senator from Pennsylvania in the first Congress, noted, "the Federalists in the first Congress were boasting that they had "cheated the People" and established a form of Government over the people which none of them expected. (Cornell, Saul, The Other Founders).

Madison spent the rest of his life trying to make amends for unleashing the power of the Federalist aristocracy. As Robert Martin noted in his recent book, Government by Dissent, "But here he was, only a few years later, no longer a Federalist, and chief legislator of the nascent opposition."

As Gordon Wood asked, "How to solve the *Madison Problem* of two Madisons?"

Even when Madison did try to ameliorate the damage he had caused by attempting to enact the Bill of Rights, he was deceitful in his support of the Bill of Rights by refusing to insert the words "expressly granted" to the enumerated Federal powers.

The phrase expressly granted was contained in the Articles of Confederation, and Madison's refusal to insert the word "expressly" in the 10th amendment was used by Justice Marshall in his ruling in McCulloch versus Maryland, 20 years later as the justification of extending federal oversight of all laws everywhere.

Like Senator Maclay, who was astonished at the Federalist' boast about pulling a fast one over the citizens, Madison eventually realized the danger of his constitution, and began to support Jefferson in fighting against the Federalist Alien and Sedition Acts of 1798, after Mason's predictions about tyranny had proven correct.

As Madison admitted, in his 1792 essay, A Candid State of Parties, "…some of the supporters of the Constitution openly or secretly attached to monarchy and aristocracy." As he noted, the Federalists had "debauched themselves into a persuasion that mankind are incapable of governing themselves, and believed that government can only be carried on by the pageantry of rank, the influence of money and emoluments, and the terror of military force."

Madison would never have had to spend this rest of his life fighting against the aristocratic Federalist tyranny, if he had not worked so closely with Hamilton in writing the Federalist Papers, and his lobbying efforts in Virginia and Pennsylvania, in getting the new constitution implemented.

Madison's constitutional arrangement was designed to check and balance the social class interests of the few and the many, not to check and balance socialism versus freedom. When both political parties failed to fulfill their historical class purposes, citizens were left with no form of representation of their natural and civil rights.

The primary political consequence of the Republican abdication of American sovereignty is that it opened a pathway for socialists to gain an electoral majority that can not be overturned, through constitutional means.

The socialists have assumed the same powerful position today in the government as the natural aristocracy obtained in 1787.

The establishment Republican Party, today, is the modern incarnation of the social class aristocracy of America's well born, and they function like a subordinate junior partner to the multiple Democrat special interest groups.

Even in the times that Republicans have a majority, they defer to the socialists.

The Democrats have the gays, the women, the environmentalists, the blacks, the latinos, all of whom benefit from the advancement of the socialist agenda. The Democrat identity special interests now comprise a voting majority of 65 million voters.

The promotion of the single Republican special interest meant "bipartisanship" with the Democrat Party's socialist agenda. This compatibility of interests between establishment Republican and left-wing Democrats is the same idea that Limbaugh calls "reaching across the aisle."

The Republican practice of reaching across the aisle is one reason why Limbaugh suggests that there should never be compromise with the socialists because every compromise means taking one step closer to the irrevocable tyrannical socialist state.

The socialist advocacy of a one-world socialist government fits within the Republican global corporate governance agenda. In other words, the reason Senator McCain, or Senator Graham, are able to reach "across the aisle" to work with Democrat socialists is that there is nothing incompatible between the socialist goals of global socialism and the Republican goals of global corporatism.

The reason that Senator McCain, Senator Graham, Paul Ryan, Marco Rubio, Jeb Bush, and John Kasich take cash from George Soros is that the globalist ambitions of Soros are not incompatible with the goals of these establishment Republican anti-Trumpers.

The Democrats agree not interfere with the globalist corporate goals of the Republicans, as long as the Democrats can impose their authoritarian tyranny on the domestic population.

The Republicans agree to the goals of the socialist state, as long as they can use the socialist state to promote global stability, across seamless national borders.

In both cases, "reaching across the aisle" means the eradication of America's natural sovereignty, in exchange for a one-world government.

Thomas Frank, the author of Listen Liberal, makes the same point about the alliance between Democrat socialists and global corporatist Republicans, in his analysis of the Democrat's abandonment of working class citizens.

In describing the elite Democrats, Frank notes that "on the matter of dealing with Wall Street, there was no conflict between idealism (of socialist Democrats) and pragmatism (of global corporate Republicans)."

What Frank is describing is the seamless alliance between socialists and global corporations, because there is no conflict between the aims of global socialism and global corporatism.

Frank meanders along to the end of his analysis of the elite socialist Democrats with his final admonition. "The course of the Democratic Party and the course of the country can both be changed, but only if we understand what the problem is."

Sadly, Frank ends his book there, without explaining what the problem is.

The problem is that neither party defends the financial and political interests of American citizens. The solution is not more socialism and centralized power in the hands of the professional elite classes that run both political parties.

The solution is to create fair constitutional rules that free up citizens to have jobs and upward mobility in a government that restricts its actions to the welfare improvement of U. S. citizens, not to citizens of the world.

What has changed in American politics is that the Democrats have abandoned their historical role of protecting non-elites, at the same time that Republicans have abandoned American sovereignty. What is new in American politics is the compatibility between the goals global socialism of Democrats, and the goals of Republicans in promoting global corporatism..

One political consequence of Madison's political arrangement causes on-going macro economic instability because it promotes elite speculation in land and assets. Speculation in land does not lead to an increase in capital investments, and in the absence of an increase in private sector investments, the economy collapses, about every 10 years.

Socialists today celebrate this speculation as much as the natural aristocracy. Joseph Stiglitz, an economic advisor to Clinton explained that, "what we were saying to the country, and to our young people, is that when we (elitist socialist Democrats) lowered the capital gains taxes and raised taxes on those who earned their living by working, is that it is far better to make your living by speculation than by any other means."

Republicans, just like socialist Democrats, are dedicated to a one-world global government using the American military to impose global order on the global market. To the Republicans, the use of military power to protect their financial interests overseas is the correct application of "ensuring domestic tranquility."

"Domestic" in this usage is the left's deconstruction for "one-world government."

The Republicans are intent to cooperate with the Democrats in order to skew the financial benefits of the American economy to themselves, using the military to enforce their global power.

This is just as Madison intended the U. S. military to be deployed for quelling the farmer's rebellions in 1785, 1792, 1835, 1888 and 1935.

The U. S. military was also very effective in extracting land from the Indians, immediately after the enactment of the Constitution.

The elites needed the Indian land for speculation, as the case of Madison's speculation of 900 acres of Indian land in New York demonstrated. At the time of the convention, Madison was engaged in Indian land speculation, primarily because he needed an independent source of wealth.

At age 36, Madison was still living with his parents. A successful land deal would provide enough wealth for him to buy his own estate. Part of his motivation at the convention in insulating the demands of the farmers from the elites was to create a better path for him to obtain the loan he needed to speculate in the Indian lands.

The corporate globalists, today, benefit from the military power that protects their interests, but they leave their profits overseas, and do not invest in America. That economic outcome of leaving their profits overseas and failing to make investments in the American economy is one reason why Republicans are as dangerous to individual freedom as the socialists.

The initial social contract of America is that all citizens would benefit from economic growth that results from a high rate of investment in the domestic economy.

For example, the explanation of the Republican behavior in promoting open-border immigration is more comprehensible when it is placed in the context of the financial interests of Big Business. Cheap labor on a global scale is vitally important to Republican Party big business donors, and granting amnesty to illegal aliens serves this goal.

The Republican lie about who they are in order to convince voters that open borders and free trade agreements, like amnesty or NAFTA, will create wealth for ordinary working class citizens.

Part of their lie creates a political subterfuge that corporate globalism is really about how free markets and free trade spread the economic benefits of growth and prosperity to all segments of the society.

Markets only perform this function of creating and spreading wealth when markets are competitive.

When markets are not competitive, in other words, when a few big corporate players dominate both the production and the sale of goods and services, markets do not perform their beneficial function of creating and distributing wealth.

This part of the Republican lie is used in a political context to justify monopoly-pricing practices of the large multinational corporations. Global monopoly pricing leads to a boom-bustglobal economic cycle because it leads to wild speculation in prices and assets.

When the boom goes bust, ordinary citizens in America suffer.

For example, the Republicans use this part of the lie to justify the high prices of gas, all the while knowing that the oil and gas industry is a huge global monopoly, sometimes called a "cartel."

There is nothing about the prices set by the global oil cartel that reflects free market price competition, yet the Republican lie is used by establishment Republicans to promote the idea that the free market is setting the price of gas.

The marginal cost of producing a barrel of oil pumped from the most extreme harsh conditions in the North Sea is about $15 per barrel. The average cost for all oil pumped from all oil fields is about $8 per barrel.

When a barrel of oil trades in the futures market for $70 per barrel, there is a "monopoly" profit of about $60 per barrel that cannot be justified or explained by free market economic theory.

When Republicans say that the high gas prices are being set in the "free market", they know that they are lying to the American public. The very last thing that the Republicans want the Federal government to deliver are free competitive markets that would set the price of oil and gas.

The second component of the Republican lie is that there is a unity of interests between the financial interests of the natural aristocracy and the natural rights of common citizens.

This idea of unity of interests was the primary political lie used by the Federalists to suggest that the new constitution did not need a Bill of Rights, since the one big consolidated central government, under the control of the natural aristocracy, would "naturally" protect the natural rights of common citizens.

The new government, the Federalists claimed, was one of specific enumerated power. All other power resided with the citizens, hence, there was no need to adopt a Bill of Rights.

In Madison's conception, the common citizens did not need to participate in the deliberations of government because the natural aristocracy would represent their interests, in a type of virtual representation.

This is the same logic used by the British, who argued that King George, and the Parliament, represented the interests of the colonists.

More and bigger government, exercised in the hands of political elites from the left is not much better than more and bigger government held in the grip of global corporations who dominate the Republican Party.

Global socialists are dedicated to using the police power of the state to impose their religious views on non-socialists. Republicans are dedicated to using the military in their neo-conservative wars to enforce open global borders.

The socialists obtained their electoral majority without a fight, because the Republicans never engaged them in an ideological war between socialism and freedom.

The Republican abdication of freedom allowed the Democrats a political opportunity to create a majority of voters by making the voters dependent on government welfare. After 1992, there was no economic growth in America, and 95 million Americans could not find jobs.

As a result of no economic growth in America, socialists now have a majority of voters. The 65 million voters who voted for Hillary will continue to vote the socialist ticket because socialism has made those voters financially dependent on government welfare.

Natural Rights Conservatives need to come to grips with the new political reality of America.

The election of Donald Trump is seen as a brief interlude in the socialist march to a majority capable of overturning the existing constitutional rules of a very weak representative republic.

Hillary got a majority of the vote, and when she lost the electoral college, the socialists immediately started claiming that Trump's victory was illegitimate.

The minority of 63 million non-socialists, who voted for Trump, are now in the exact inferior political position as the wealthy bond holders were in 1787, when Madison vowed to protect the minority of wealthy bond owners from the majority of farmers in the state legislatures.

Madison's phrase for this part of his scheme was to protect minority interests from the democratic majority interests. In creating his system, he eradicated the common citizen's rights to over-ride the authority of the central government.

When the socialists are successful in taking over the central government, there is nothing stopping them from permanently imposing their special form of slavery on the non-socialists. They will take over the institutional mechanisms of power designed by Madison for the natural elite.

The Federalists believed that common citizens could not be trusted to make decisions, and therefore, the aristocratic elites should have all the power to make decisions.

The central tenant of the socialist religion is that the minority of socialist elites are much smarter than the citizens, and therefore, the socialist elites should have all the constitutional power to make decisions.

The new socialist majority will never stop trying to de-legitimize Trump because they do not believe in natural rights, the rule of law, or the principles of democratic representation.

Part of the socialist strategy in de-legitimizing the election of Trump is to get rid of the electoral college, and replace it with a majority vote for President. When Supreme Court Justice Ginsberg openly promotes the elimination of the electoral college, this is part of the left's strategy of de-legitimizing Trump.

The anti-Trump Republicans will never stop their rantings against Trump, because they know that Trump is not an establishment Republican, and he is not an advocate of global corporatism.

A much better idea for the natural rights conservatives, beginning after the 2008 election, would have been to abandon the Republican Party, in favor of creating a political party whose goal is the protection of citizen natural rights.

The primary political consequence of the Republican abdication of freedom is that it ushered into American society the prospect of an alien socialist ideology that despises the tenets of natural rights individualism. If, and when, the socialists gain the institutional mechanisms of power in Madison's constitutional British class system, the Republicans can not be counted on to help common citizens restore their natural rights.

Like the scene in the movie, Braveheart, when Wallace confronted the King on the field of battle, and had relied on the Scottish nobility to assist him in the ensuing battle of Scottish independence, the Republicans can be expected to turn away from the battle, in favor of protecting their privileges of monarchy.

As this book will detail, the Republicans are unreliable, as allies in the battle against socialist tyranny, and are untruthful about their allegiance to the constitutional principles of natural rights.

As a direct result of the two-party class system Madison created, natural rights conservatives do not have a legitimate democratic option to choose liberty in any federal election.

One party, that was supposed to represent the interests of common citizens, has turned into the global socialist party.

The other party, that was supposed to be virtuous, abandoned its allegiance to the sovereignty of the nation.

Madison locked the citizens into his two party system, and they can not undo his damage. The Democrats have colluded with Republicans to pass laws that eliminate alternatives to the two party duopoly, and those laws have been upheld by the courts.

Those laws include barriers to ballot access, campaign financing hurdles, gerrymandering, exclusion from debates, voter fraud, and media blackouts.

The consequence of Madison's flawed arrangement is neither a representative republic based upon the rule of law nor a system of government, based on the based on the natural rights of the consent of the governed.

It is a centralized global tyranny, operated for the benefit of the global elites, against the many.

As explained by Merrill Jensen, in his book, Articles of Confederation, what the anti-federalist did not see, in 1781, was that the conservatives had learned a bitter lesson in their efforts to create a national government in 1777.

Jensen writes, "…the nationalists adopted a theory of the sovereignty of the people, in the name of the people, and erected a nationalistic government whose purpose was to thwart the will of the people in whose name they acted…"

In turn, Jensen explains that what the nationalists failed to see, in 1787, was that the government that they had created may be captured by the socialists on a national scale.

This is exactly the outcome that Mason predicted, except that he did not anticipate that it would be a socialist tyranny that captured the central government.

"Sometimes, achieving an efficient outcome requires the winners of free trade to compensate the losers," said Kevin Kliesen, an economist with the St. Louis Federal Reserve Bank in his article, *Trading Barbs: A Primer on the Globalization Debate.*

After his review of the standard operating assumptions in favor of global trade, he adds the important caveat that he takes from another branch of economics called welfare economic theory.

He notes that the great increase in profits for corporations that have resulted from the offshoring of American innovation may require the corporate winners of global trade to provide some compensation to all the Americans who have lost their jobs and their incomes.

"Estimates of the net benefits that flow from free trade are substantial," notes Kliesen. "International trade has increased real household income by between $7,000 and $13,000 since the end of WWII, according to a study by economists Scott Bradford, Paul Grieco and Gary Hufbauer," (The Regional Economist, October 2007).

Kliesen's reference to "household" income could be somewhat confusing for non-economists, who would see the words, real household income, and assume that the words meant family household income, not corporate profits.

However, the way that economists use the term, national income includes both wages and salaries and corporate profits. Wages have gone down, but profits have shot up since 2002, as a result of changes in U. S. trade and tax policies.

Diagram 1.1 Trends In Corporate Profit Rates Following Offshoring

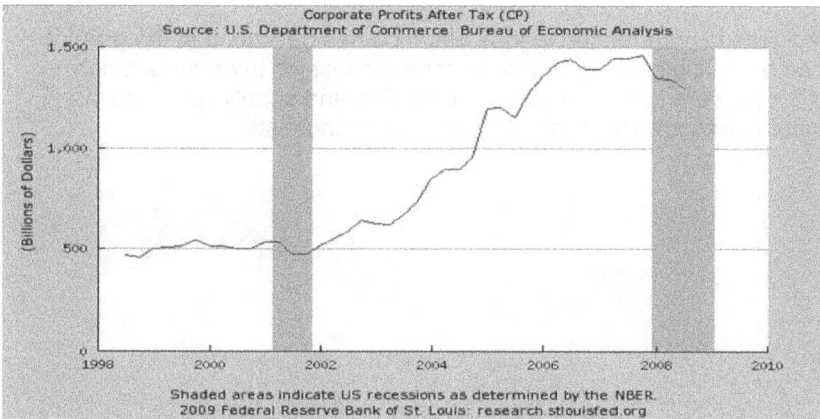

The rising tide of corporate profits from global trade policies are not flowing to the wages and salaries of American families, and therefore, Kliesen calls upon another branch of economic theory to suggest that the winners (multi

national corporations) may need to compensate the losers of global trade (everyone else in the American society).

Economists call this type of compensation, where the winners, theoretically, compensate the losers, the Pareto Compensation Principle.

It is not necessary for actual real dollars to be paid by the winners to the losers. The economic justification of the Republican trade and tax policies would work out, in theory, if there is enough of an increase in the profit part of national household income, so that the winners could, theoretically, compensate the losers.

One big difference in economic policy between socialists and global corporate Republicans is that a socialist, like Obama, uses the power of government to extract taxes from the middle class in order to compensate the losers.

Since 2008, under Obama, income transfers increased from 35% of total government expenditures to 55%. The increase in welfare payments served to create the majority of socialist voters in the 2016 election.

Republicans generally prefer just to point out that the winners could, theoretically, compensate the losers, without actually doing anything about the growing income inequality caused by their trade policies.

Corporations are not paying the increased tax burdens of the increased income transfers implemented by the socialists, even though the global corporations are causing an economic disaster for the American middle class.

As a part of the enactment of the Republican trade policies, corporations were granted Congressional authority to actively shift income around the world, to avoid paying high U.S. tax rates.

When global profits do not flow back into the U. S. domestic economy, the U. S. economy suffers a massive loss of jobs for middle class citizens.

The direct loss in manufacturing jobs and incomes described in the graphic below can be multiplied by 2, because for each lost job in manufacturing, another 2 jobs were lost indirectly in the service and supply value chains, called income and employment multipliers by economists.

Diagram 1.2 The Direct Loss in Manufacturing Jobs Since 1998

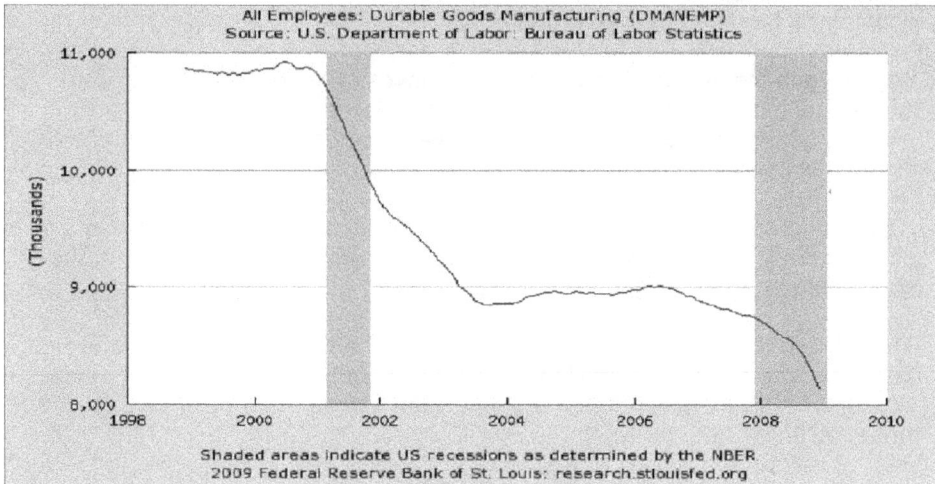

The primary job losses are a result of companies that no longer exist. When profits do not flow back into the domestic economy, small businesses that depend on large corporations to buy supplies, go bankrupt.

It appears that the number of U. S. manufacturing firms that have gone out of business since 2004 is about 100,000.

In her report to Congress on Federal programs that support industrial competitiveness, Wendy Schacht cites 350,000 small U. S. manufacturing establishments in 2004. *(Cooperative R&D: Federal Efforts to Promote Industrial Competitiveness*, CRS Report For Congress, Updated August 20, 2008).

The most recent CRS report at the end of 2008, shows that the comparable number of small manufacturing establishments in the U. S. was about 250,000.

During that same period of time, (2004 to 2008), the number of small manufacturing establishments in Wake County, North Carolina, dropped from around 500 to under 200. (Telephone survey by author conducted in July 2008).

As a result of the Republican Party global trade policies, Michael Porter, at the Harvard Business School has summarized the macro economic consequences of the trade policies.

Median real household income has declined 7%, since 1999, with incomes stagnating across virtually all income levels. Despite a welcome jump in 2015, median household income remains below the peak attained in 1999, 17 years ago.

Between the 1970s and the 1990s, the U.S. economy created private-sector jobs at a long-run rate of roughly 2% per year decade after decade. The job growth rate began to decline around 2001.

Beginning in the late 1990s, private sector investment for equipment, intellectual property and structures began to decline. For 2010–2016,the average quarterly investment by business as a percentage of GDP was lower than it has been since the 1980s.

Had workforce participation stayed at the level seen in 1997, current levels of employment in America would imply an unemployment rate of 11.1% for the working-age population (ages 16–64).

The number of small business firms created in the U.S. was actually lower in 2010 than the number of small business that went bankrupt. The total number of businesses with fewer than 500 employees has declined by more than 5%, since 1999.

Half of the country's new business establishments created between 2010 and 2014 were clustered in just 20 counties, in the nation.

Since 2000, large global corporations, with more than 1,000 employees, have grown jobs much faster than businesses with fewer than 100 employees. The job growth is concentrated in just 20 counties, in the nation.

Porter asks, "Why are large companies and their owners and managers thriving even as working- and middle-class workers and small businesses struggle? For their success, many large companies rely on access to innovation, capital, and high-quality management."

Porter explains why global corporations are doing so well, since 1992. "The ensuing globalization and technological progress," explained Porter, greatly benefited American firms." Porter could have added the clarification that it was large global firms that benefited from the trade policies.

Porter added, "globalization and technological change have put pressure on the U.S. economy and especially on working- and middle-class Americans and consumers."

Between 2001, the year before the enactment of the trade and tax laws, U. S. corporate direct investment abroad was $119 billion. At the end of 2004, it was $219.8 billion.

In other words, one consequence of the Republican trade laws on U.S. economic growth has been to divert about $100 billion in capital investments to other countries, in a 3 year period.

Since 2002, the rate of business investment in America, especially in the nine high technology value chains, has declined dramatically. Without a flow of investment capital from corporate profits back into domestic U. S. economy, there is no economic growth in America.

Since 1992, however, U. S. corporations with foreign operations have primarily invested their profits overseas.

The minimum **required** rate of investment in U.S. corporations just to keep the domestic economy **running-in-place**, and maintain the status quo is about $100 billion per year, about the same magnitude of the increase in foreign investment made by global corporations, over that same period of time.

Running in place means that the level of investment is just enough to replace and replenish the existing capital stock of machinery and equipment in production plants. Running in place does not produce economic growth, and, in the absence of economic growth, citizens are attracted to the siren song of socialism.

The economic term used to describe the level of investment to run in place is "capital consumption adjustment." The American economy does not even have the level of investment required to run in place.

The rate of corporate investment in America has dropped dramatically since the enactment of the new trade and tax policies of 2002. The large corporations have no need to make investments in the U. S. domestic economy because their new capital stock is over in India.

When the minimum required level of capital investment is not made, the economy ratchets down to a new lower level of economic activity.

Some economists call this new lower level of equilibrium the "new normal."

Other economists call this same idea a "Nash Equilibrium," which describes an economic condition of very low output, that is none-the-less, a stable equilibrium. In historical economic terms, this low level equilibrium was the issue being addressed by Lord Keynes in the mid-1930s. Economic theory at the time, suggested that this low level of output was inconsistent with reality.

Diagram 1.3 Trends In the Minimal Rates of Investment Just To Run-In-Place

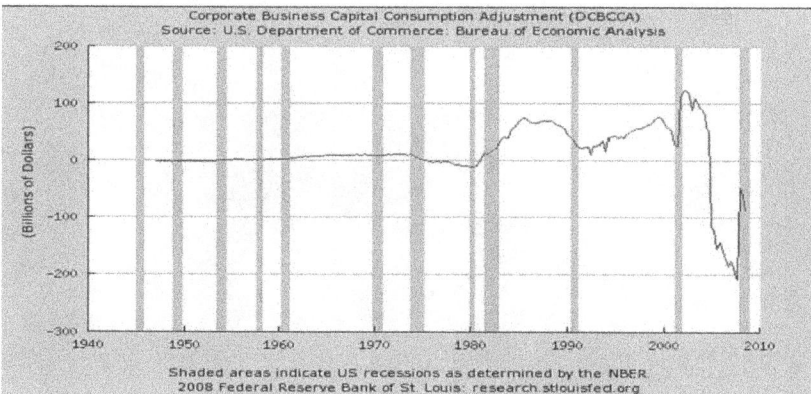

The key variable in the innovation equation for job creation is profit reinvestment, primarily in new small high tech ventures.

Corporate profits earned from their overseas operations are not taxed until they are converted back into U.S. currency. As long as the profits can be delayed in conversion to the U. S. currency, the U. S. tax obligations can be evaded.

Majority-owned foreign affiliates of U.S. MNCs (henceforth, foreign affiliates) performed $27.5 billion in R&D abroad in 2004 after adjusting for inflation, up $4.7 billion or 17.4% from 2003, which was the largest annual increase since a 22% rise in 1999.

In general, changes in foreign direct investment in foreign research and development is directly the result of the trade policies in 1992 and 2002.

"The high price of 'free' trade," notes Robert E. Scott, "results from a set of guarantees designed to stimulate foreign direct investment and the movement of factories within the hemisphere, especially from the United States to Canada and Mexico. NAFTA contained a number of unique provisions designed to provide special protections for investors in order to encourage foreign direct investment in chapter eleven of the agreement, which concerned investment." (EPI Briefing Paper #147, November 17, 2003.)

Chapter 2. The Consequence of the Republican Trade Policies on Job Creation

As the recent research by the Business Dynamics Statistical agency show, the loss of all manufacturing establishments, after 1992, entailed a huge loss of jobs, which have not been offset, either by jobs from the birth of new establishments, or by jobs created by the global corporations.

What changed, after 1992, was that the historical job creation dynamic at work in America had stopped working. Small, new ventures were not creating jobs fast enough to compensate for the loss of jobs in the older bigger corporations. (*Business Formation and Dynamics by Business Age: Results from the New Business Dynamics Statistics,* John Haltiwanger, Ron Jarmin and Javier Miranda, May 2008 Preliminary Draft).

The bifurcation in the American economy resulting from offshoring can be seen in their graphic 2.1 below. The American rate of job creation from new ventures is too low, and the birth rate of new ventures is too low to offset the loss of jobs from the trade policies.

Diagram 2.1 The Rate of Job Destruction vs. Job Creation

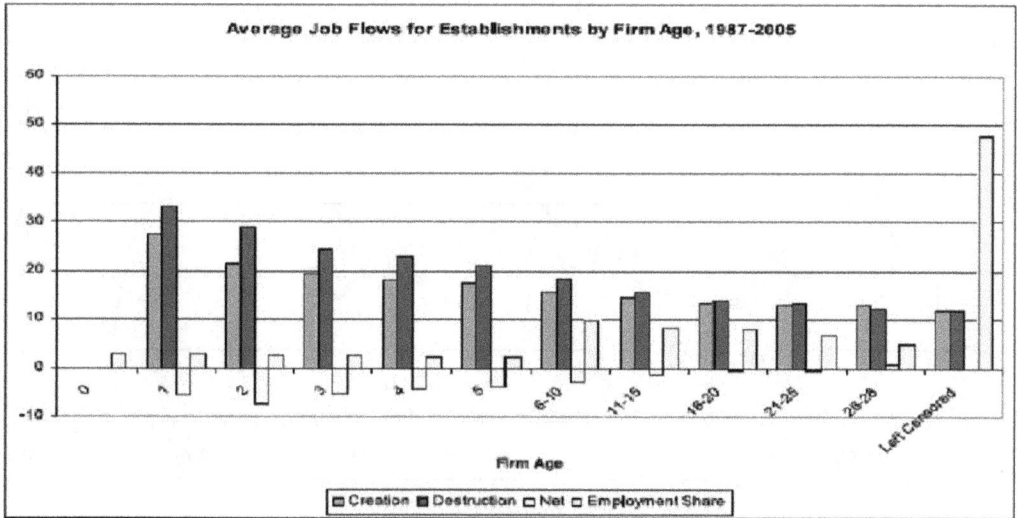

Average Job Flows for Establishments by Firm Age, 1987-2005

They state, "The implied contribution of business formation is very substantial especially in light of the average overall net growth of employment for this period of about 1.8 percent per year. Compared to the 3 percent number, this suggests that all other firms taken together were a net drag on the economy in terms of job growth of about -1.2 percent. Put differently, the U.S. economy is constantly reinventing itself– on net adding jobs but doing so through business formation (new firms) with existing firms on average contracting."

The major job losses in America, since 2002, are in the older, larger global firms, who are engaged in offshoring. When they offshore, they destroy jobs in America. The rate of job loss in the older firms is greater than the rate of job creation in new firms. And, the rate of new venture creation in America is headed down.

They continue, "About 1/3 of the annual job creation rate is due to establishment entry. The very high rate of gross job creation is balanced with a very high rate of gross job destruction. The gross job destruction rate is around 16 percent on average indicated that about 16 percent of jobs that existed one year prior no longer exist."

For the past 30 years, (starting around 1987), the political system in America has not addressed the fundamental structural labor market weaknesses created by the Republican trade policies.

Diagram 2.2. Job Gains and Losses

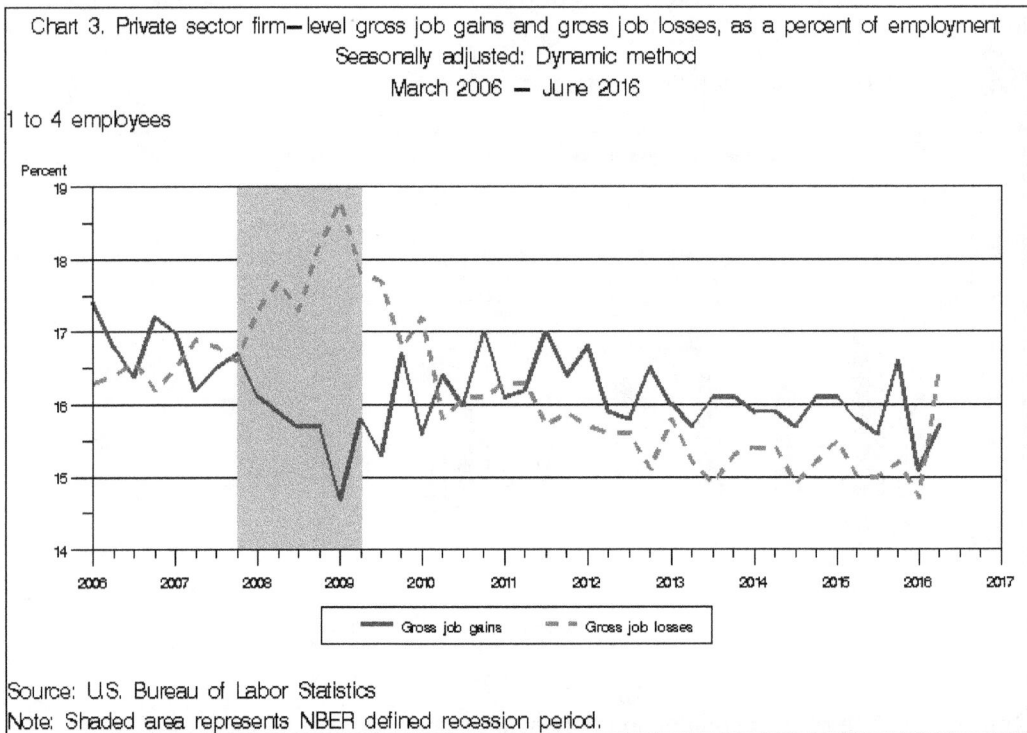

Chart 3. Private sector firm—level gross job gains and gross job losses, as a percent of employment
Seasonally adjusted: Dynamic method
March 2006 — June 2016

Source: U.S. Bureau of Labor Statistics
Note: Shaded area represents NBER defined recession period.

Part of the issue is that Republican leaders abandoned their allegiance to the rule of law. When Justice Roberts rules that a penalty fee in ObamaCare is actually a tax, and that Congress has the power to tax, but does not have the authority to impose penalty fees for not buying a product, Roberts abandons the rule of law.

Part of the issue is that there has not been job growth, and without job growth, common citizens do not have allegiance to the rule of law, just like Hillary and Obama did not have allegiance to the rule of law.

Job growth, upward occupational mobility, and a rate of GDP economic growth of around 4% per year, caused by private investments, are absolutely essential to the functioning of a natural rights republic.

The recent economic collapse in September of 2008 was caused by government monetary and fiscal policy that created a series of government-induced speculative bubbles in bonds and real estate.

The Fed's abysmal management of the interest rate has made the consequences of the economic collapse much worse than it would have been without the Fed's manipulation of money supply and interest rates.

In traditional economic theory, the level of aggregate investment is a function of interest rates. As interest rates dropped after 2008, investment should have increased. If investment had increased, following the advice of Lord Keynes, there should have been job growth in America from 1997 to 2017.

The Federal Reserve, beginning around 1997, coordinated U. S. national monetary policy with other central banks, as a part of the globalization in monetary policy. In other words, the financial beneficiaries of the Federal Reserve zero interest rates are primarily foreign banks, not the increased welfare of common citizens in the U. S.

When the U. S. Treasury and the Fed bailed out the banks after the 2008 collapse, most of the banks that were bailed out were foreign banks.

The Fed's main response for banks in the U. S. domestic economy was to force consolidation of many big banks into many fewer big banks.

In other words, in the most fundamental sense, after 2008, the Fed acted to enhance the power of monopoly capital for the benefit of the well born, by consolidating the banking system into fewer and fewer hands.

The type of global trade policies promoted by the Republicans, and endorsed by the Democrats, served to benefit a very small segment of the American society, and the benefits of that type of global trade were not distributed widely across all sectors of society.

The cause of the labor market failure, after 1992, was the Republican sponsored government policies that resulted in the massive structural transformation of the labor market from a jobs creation machine to a welfare dependency society, where over 95 million workers are defined as "not in the labor force."

The responsibility for this outcome of permanent unemployment for 95 million workers, are the Republican trade and tax policies, not Democrat income transfer policies.

Obama, and the socialists, made the economic problems worse, but Democrats did not initially cause the problems related to global trade policies enacted in the 1990 to 2002 period.

As a result of enactment of new Republican global trade agreements and U.S. tax policies in 1992 and 2002 that favor direct foreign investment (FDI) over domestic investment, the American economy has "bifurcated."

The pace of offshoring increased dramatically after 2002, with increased rates of engineering and scientific functions related to innovation being shipped overseas, primarily to India.

The speculative bubbles, after 2002, were induced by banking and fiscal policies that the Republican Party enacted to ameliorate the economic consequences of global trade on American workers who did not benefit from the global trade policies.

The consequence of the global trade policies was to destroy the American job creation machine, which is one reason why the economic recession of 2008 has had a "jobless" recovery.

The Fed's fiscal and tax policies, such as Quantitative Easing, were an attempt at using government to have the winners in global trade compensate the losers, with welfare payments and money creation, which created the speculative bubbles.

Obama made the economic collapse much worse with his squandering of $800 billion in his fake stimulus package, which served to bind socialist special interests to the Democrat Party.

But, Obama did not cause the speculative collapse in real estate bonds in September of 2008.

Table 2.3 provides the chronology of financial and economic events, from 1987 to 2008, to describe how the economic problems caused by the U. S. Federal Reserve Bank created the series of speculative economic bubbles.

The chronology describes the events that occurred during the transition to a global market, which accelerated as a result of the Republican trade policies in 1992 and 2002.

Diagram 2.3. Chronology of Economic Collapses Caused by Speculation

September 2008 Mortgage Debt Bubble Bursts. U. S. Economy Collapses.	Speculative economic and financial markets did not create conditions of long-term economic growth. Government intervention and spending does not create lasing benefits because domestic markets and economy are no longer integrated. Foreclosures reach historic highs. Bankruptcies
March 2008 Oil and Gas Prices Begin Speculative Increase From $43 per barrel to $145 per barrel.	Speculation and market collusion between oil corporations and government officials. Increase oil prices sucks the life out of consumer spending. Consumer spending dramatically declines in final demand market. Circuit City files Chapter 7
2003 – 2008 U. S. Rate of Job Creation Lower than Rate of Job Destruction.	Offshoring of U. S. R&D innovation creates Bifurcated domestic economy. A large part of the domestic economy does not benefit from transactions in the global value chains. Regional

2004 U. S. Rates of Profit for 1500 Largest MNCs Located in U. S. Increase to Record Levels	Profits not reinvested in U. S. domestic value chains, reinvested in foreign global value chains
2003 U. S. Rate of Domestic Direct Investment Declines. U. S. Foreign Direct Investment	Platform for U.S. R&D and new product development shifts to India and China
2002 U. S. Trade and Tax Policies Changed to Facilitate Offshoring of Innovation and R&D. Changes in regulation of corporations leads to Enron-type collapses and wide-spread corporate	Engineering and professional jobs lost in U.S. Consumer and investor confidence in the integrity of the financial markets begins to erode. "Rule of Law" routinely evaded by financial and political elites.
September 11, 2001 Terrorists Attack US.	Stock market collapses again. U. S. economy enters recession.
March 2001 IT/IPO Bubble Bursts.	The investments made during 1999 to 2001 mostly in IT, did not create future economic demand and new markets in 2008. A generation
1997 Speculative IPO Bubble Begins.	Capital gains and profits from the exits in IT investments made in 1992 are ploughed back into to speculative early stage investments. Speculation and collusion in the IPO market dumps hundreds of worthless IT companies into
1985 – 1992 Changes in tax and trade policies leads to increased rate of production jobs lost due to	Metro Regional Value Chains, Interindustry Linkages Destroyed. Loss of employment and income multipliers. Production that used to be
1991 Speculative real estate bubble and LBO bubble both burst causing recession of 1991.	Profits from real estate speculation and LBO bubble were not re-invested in ventures that created long term economic growth. American economy begins to enter the series of speculative bubbles caused by government banking policy
October 19, 1987 Black Monday Stock Market Crash.	Collusion, speculation, insider trading and program trading cause the first big stock market crash that sets the course of the U. S. economy for the next 30 years.

This same type of economic analysis of the effect of speculation could be used to explain all of the economic collapses for the entire U. S. economic history, since the enactment of Madison's flawed arrangement.

The anti-federalists of 1787, the anti-monopoly Jacksonians of 1837, the agrarian populists of 1888, all suffered, needlessly, as a result of the speculative bubbles, and the monetary policies caused by the Central Bank.

All of these groups made exactly the same, accurate, arguments about what caused the economic distress in their own historical epoch. The cause of the distress is unfair constitutional rules that results in the lack of jobs and the lack of upward occupational mobility.

Over and over again, the common citizens have rebelled against the unfair and non-uniform application of fair rules of competition contained in Madison's flawed arrangement. The financial results of the unfair rules do not have moral legitimacy. The centralized authority does not function to grant individual liberty, as promised in the original Articles of Confederation.

The response of the American government throughout history to the economic instability has been to favor the financial interests of the well born over the interests of common citizens. In exchange for this political bargain, the virtuous elite engage in speculative ventures and offshore production facilities.

In most cases the financial policies enacted had the double benefit for the well born, because the central banks policies caused farmers to lose their land in legal debt-lien laws, the proximate cause of which are Madison's unbalanced system of checks and balances, contained in Article I, Section 10 of his constitution.

As a result of the trade policies, the American economy has a permanent job creation deficit. The main reason the American labor force participation rate has declined so sharply during the 2008 economic downturn is that for the past 27 years, the job creation rate has fallen below the job destruction rate, while the labor force continues to grow.

Diagram 2.4. The Rate of Job Destruction vs. Job Creation by Firm Size

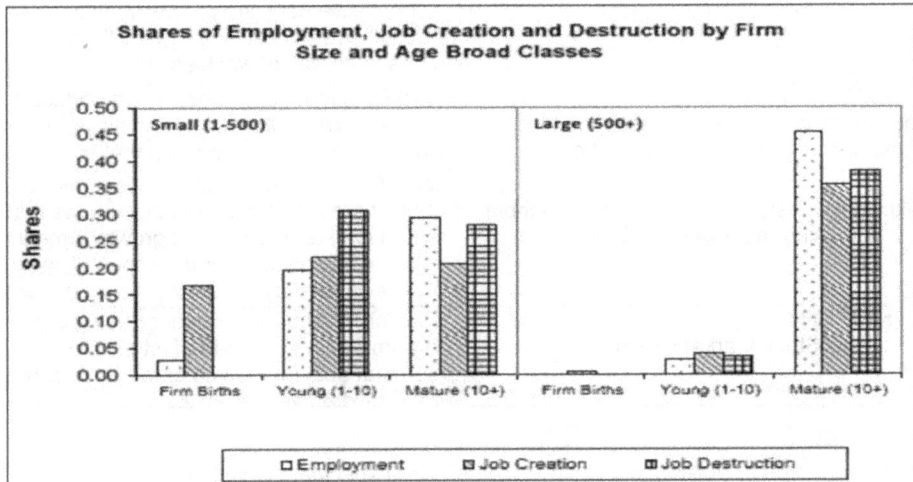

Shares of Employment, Job Creation and Destruction by Firm Size and Age Broad Classes

As a result of the low levels of job creation, jobs are very difficult to find. Those without work stay unemployed longer, driving up the unemployment rate.

Diagram 2.5 describes the duration of unemployment, after 2002. In this period of time, the U. S. economy was "running-in-place" and the duration of during that time was around 10 weeks. After the real estate bubble collapse in 2008, the duration of unemployment increased to around 20 weeks.

Recent labor market statistics indicate that the job search intensity of the long-term unemployed increases, after around 35 weeks. The unemployed are desperate to find a job.

After about 60 weeks of unemployment, the unemployed simply give up and drop out of the labor force. There are currently around 95 million American workers who have stopped searching for work.

After about 60 weeks of not finding a job, many of these welfare dependent citizens turn to the political promises of the socialists.

Diagram 2.5. Job Search Duration

Chart 1. **Median duration of unemployment for persons who became employed or left the labor force in the subsequent month, not seasonally adjusted 12-month moving average, January 1995–December 2010**

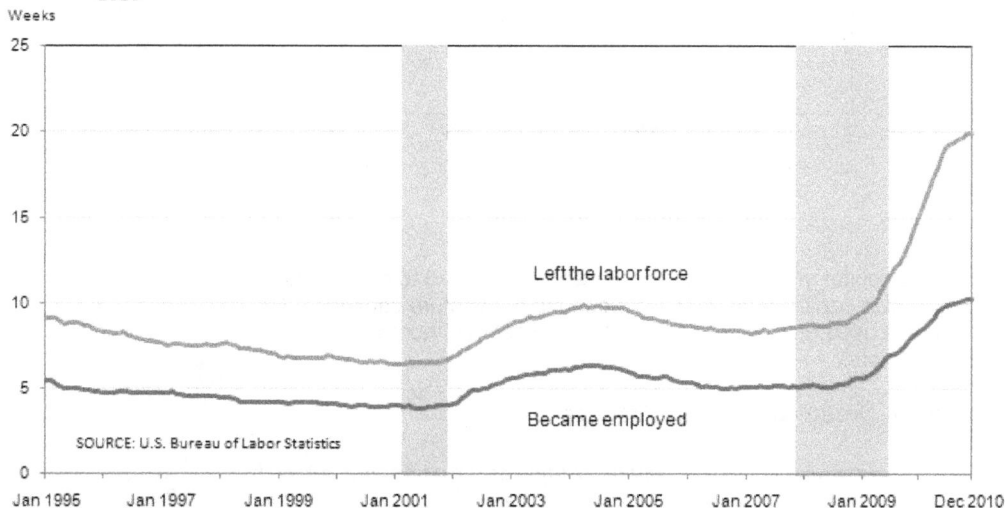

Weeks

Left the labor force

Became employed

SOURCE: U.S. Bureau of Labor Statistics

Jan 1995 Jan 1997 Jan 1999 Jan 2001 Jan 2003 Jan 2005 Jan 2007 Jan 2009 Dec 2010

NOTE: Shaded areas represent recessions as determined by the National Bureau of Economic Research (NBER). Duration is based on the number of weeks unemployed in the month before becoming employed or leaving the labor force and, therefore, is somewhat understated.

As a result of the structural economic changes related to offshoring, the birth rate of new business firms is the same as the death rate of older businesses. Prior to 2002, new businesses were the source of most job creation but the older companies are laying off many more jobs than the new companies are creating.

After 2002, whatever jobs that have been created in the domestic U. S. economy, have primarily been created by corporations that have over 1000 workers.

Most jobs, prior to 2002, were created by very small new firms with less than 100 employees. It takes about 3 years for most new small firms to reach 9 employees.

The most important time for job growth is when the new firm enters its 6th year, but the private capital markets in America have stopped funding both new ventures and firms that need growth capital in the 5th year.

Diagram 2.6. Establishment Entry and Exit, Employment Weighted:

Chart 1: **Aggregate entry and exit rates have been declining**
Annual data

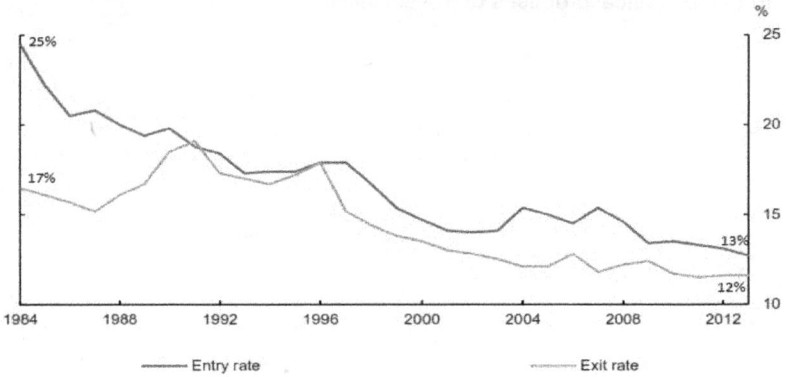

The private capital markets in America are not organized to provide the needed growth capital in the 6th year, because the venture capitalists, like all elites, are focused on funding a speculative investment home run that returns 800% in 2 years.

Diagram 2.7. Net Job Creation By Firm Age

Net private-sector employment changes by firm age, years ending in March 2000–15

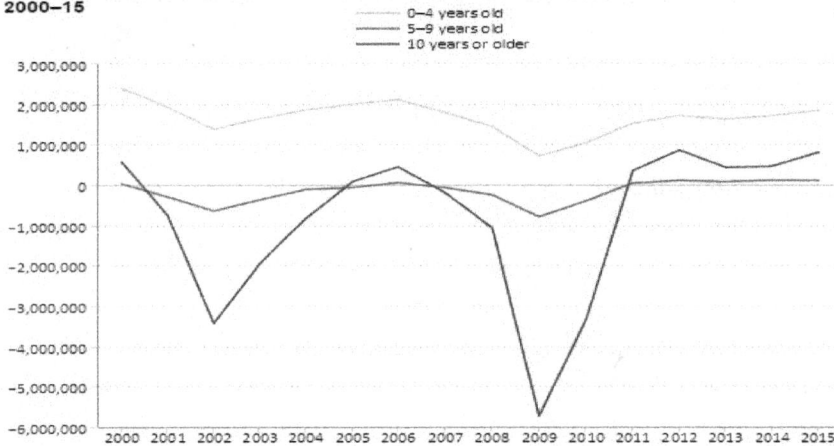

Source: U.S. Bureau of Labor Statistics.

After 2008, the rate of job creation in new small firms was not great enough to offset the loss of American jobs in older bigger corporations. The large older firms were shedding about 4 million jobs per year. The new firms were creating about 1 million jobs per year.

The greater risk of job loss as a result of the structural economic changes in the American economy related to the tax laws and trade agreements has caused great anxiety and insecurity among American workers.

Diagram 2.8. Trends In Citizen Economic Insecurity Following Offshoring

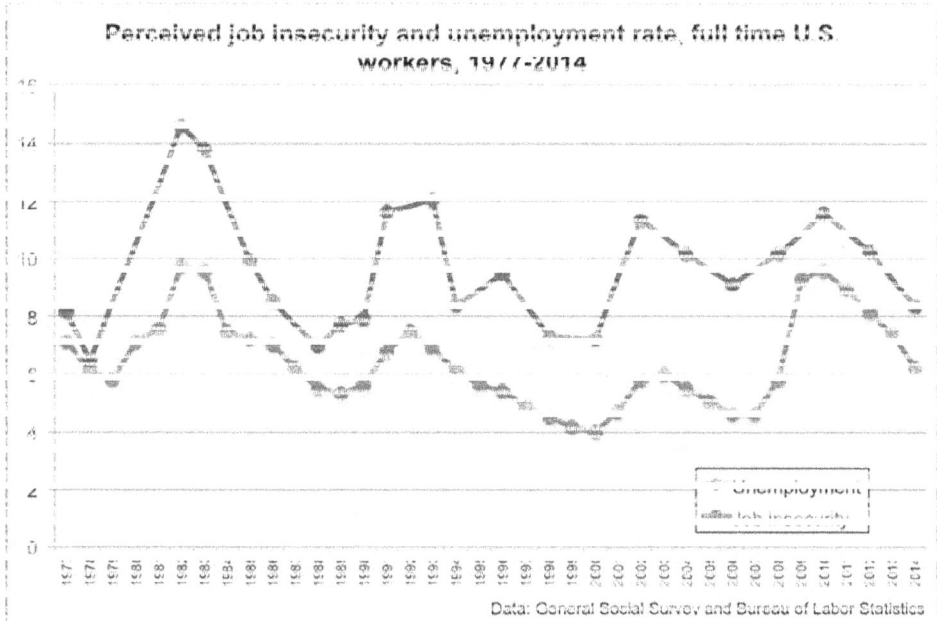

Perceived job insecurity and unemployment rate, full time U.S. workers, 1977-2014

Data: General Social Survey and Bureau of Labor Statistics

The loss of confidence and trust in the American economic and financial systems has been cited by economists as the proximate cause of the American economic collapse in September of 2008.

The loss of trust in America is also a proximate cause of the rise of socialism, and the growing socialist voting majority, leading to a majority vote of 65 million voters for Hillary, in 2016.

In a natural rights republic, common citizens must have jobs, or they lose their allegiance to the rule of law and begin voting the socialist ticket.

On the other hand, the new trade laws are benefiting large corporations.

Cisco, for example, recently established Cisco Center East in Bangalore, India, as the new Cisco corporate headquarters for companywide *innovation*, under the leadership of the first chief globalization officer of the company. Their former San Jose–based U.S. headquarters is now referred to as Cisco

Center West, reflecting its new role in the corporation. Cisco's rate of profits during the recent U. S. economic collapse have been very high.

Cisco now has 2,000 people doing R&D in India. The jobs for highly skilled, highly-paid workers used to be located in America.

Diagram 2.9. Cisco Income Statement

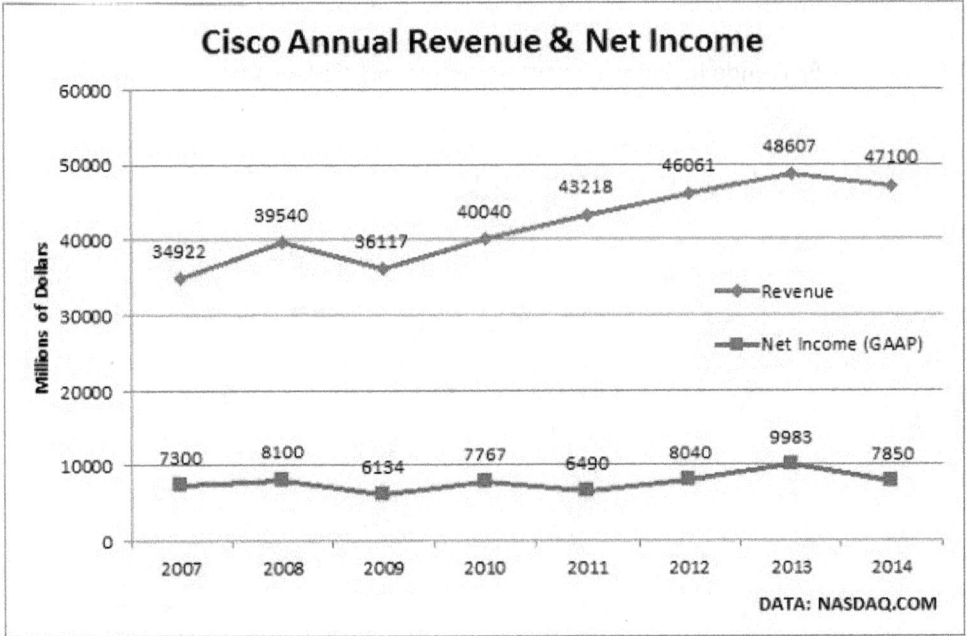

Cisco Annual Revenue & Net Income

Year	Revenue	Net Income (GAAP)
2007	34922	7300
2008	39540	8100
2009	36117	6154
2010	40040	7767
2011	43218	6490
2012	46061	8040
2013	48607	9983
2014	47100	7850

DATA: NASDAQ.COM

Individual freedom provides the framework for the free competitive markets to function. In the chronology of events leading to the formation of a natural rights republic, God grants citizens freedom.

Citizens form governments to protect their freedoms. One of their God-given freedoms is property. Property, protected by government comes first, and then after the protection of property, come free markets, which create the greatest individual and national wealth.

Free markets and free citizens depend on the rule of law to function as a part of a free society.

Property, in a natural rights republic, acts as the adhesive glue that binds citizens to obey the rule of law. In forming their government, citizens agree to obey the laws that they give to themselves.

In the case of America, the great mass of common citizens did not have real estate property. Their labor was their property, and Jefferson, following Locke, had guaranteed that citizens were entitled to the fruits of their labor-property.

Madison's flawed arrangement made this part of the rule of law unbalanced in favor of the well born, who obtained political power to control economic growth. Rather than make investments that cause future economic growth, the well born have engaged in 250 years of commodity and land speculation.

Commodity and land speculation causes economic collapse in America about every 10 years, or so.

What changed in America, after 1992, is the conversion of the Democratic Party, from its initial political representation of common citizens, into a socialistic political movement that is outside the national historic consensus that the purpose of Madison's arrangement was to balance the interests of the common citizens against the interests of the elite.

What changed in America, after 1992, is the abandonment of liberty, by the Republican Party, in favor of extending their own form of elite tyranny in a global one-world government.

Chapter 3: The Consequence of the Republican Abdication of Freedom On American Ingenuity and Technological Innovation

In a natural rights republic, it is individual freedom that allows entrepreneurs to make money in the future time period from the risky investments that they make in the current time period. Part of this idea is based in Jefferson's notion that citizens own their own labor, and have a natural right to use their labor to create their own happiness.

Without the social framework of individual freedom, entrepreneurs are not confident that they will be able to reap their future rewards, and without the risky investments, there is no technological innovation.

In other words, there is an important relationship between constitutional rights, and the rate of technological innovation in a natural rights republic.

Without technological innovation, there is no economic growth. Without economic growth, there is no upward occupational mobility. Without upward occupational mobility, America does not have the glue that holds disassociated individuals together.

This chapter explains the relationship between technological innovation and economic growth, which is caused by the creation of new future markets.

When the Republicans abandoned the defense of freedom, American citizens lost their most important competitive advantage over European and Asian collectivist and socialist societies. The initial factor endowment of individual ingenuity made America's economy different than any other nation.

The non-economic term for American technological superiority is sometimes called "American ingenuity." It is also sometimes referred to, in non-economic documents, as the American cultural value of "self-made" citizens.

The Republican trade and tax policies abdicated freedom in such a way as to make technological innovation the exclusive province of the large corporations, to the detriment of small firms and entrepreneurs.

In abdicating freedom, the Republicans served to destroy the American economy of self-made citizens, and replaced it with a society dependent on either global corporations, or the socialists.

Because of the way that Republicans abdicated freedom, there is no longer a growing middle class of self-made, independent citizens in America.

The sequence of events leading to dissipating America's technological superiority began in the late 1980s. The initial set of Republican trade policies began an era of outsourcing production in goods. The goods were made in overseas manufacturing plants, and then imported into America.

Over time the outsourcing of production led to outsourcing of scientific research and development in new products.

The sequence of events took place over a 20-year period of time. The most damaging policies were adopted in 1992 and 2002.

Global corporations initially sought out certain regional metropolitan markets in foreign countries in order to obtain market advantage in production, but more importantly, to learn about new methods of production and new ideas for products.

Some scholars, notably from the organizational information theory school, have looked at this non-symmetrical relationship between corporations and regional elected representatives, and concluded as Wigand, et. al., did in *Information, Organization and Management*, that "...regional or national borders play a decreasingly important role for the definition and organization of corporate economic activity."

In their view, the new global "boundary-less" corporation will become the main economic actor in a borderless global market. In other words, cities and nations will not matter to corporations as distinct sovereign political units, but will matter as distinct technological assets that can potentially contribute to the corporation's competitive objectives.

Rod Coombs and his colleagues, who studied the issue of technological innovation, found a high number of innovations that were made in the social business network of scientists in a distinct geographical place. As they noted in *Economics and Technological Change*, "...there is evidence from a number of studies to suggest that many of the important scientific ideas in the life of an innovation come from outside the innovating company, via these channels of professional scientific communication."

One goal of the global outsourcing for the senior corporate managers is to internally absorb the regional innovation that occurs in other parts of the world.

In order for the entire global corporate management system to absorb technological innovation, every metro region must look like and act like every other region. This global uniformity is one outcome of how the Republicans implemented their global trade policies.

The consequence was to make the 350 American metro regions look and function, politically, just like all the socialist and collectivist metro regions in the world, with the concomitant loss of the most important initial factor of endowment: American individual ingenuity and initiative.

When senior executives or Republicans use the phrase "American workers must be globally competitive" this is the same way of saying that American workers must compete at the same wage levels of other nations.

Prior to 1980, senior corporate managers could not overcome the local customs and laws in other nations, and they did not dare risk making their intentions clear to the U. S. public. Their main difficulty in managing global operations was a communication technology barrier because they could not make operations uniform and standardized across national borders and regional boundaries.

Beginning around 1980, the new information communication technology (ICT) allowed senior corporate management to achieve global market uniformity and inter-operational standardization, so that they could begin treating their branch operations in every region like operations in every other region.

Once the internet technologies of the late 1980s solved their global communication issues, the senior executives needed the additional political and legal framework, enacted in 1992 and 2002, to make the new ICT work for them.

As explained by James Simmie, in *Innovation and Agglomeration Theory*, "the world map for multinational corporations looks like a series of places ranked by ...different roles in the international division of labor."

Uniformity and standardization are the antithesis to individual diversity and creativity that fosters American individualistic technological innovation. Regional uniformity, from an international economic trade perspective, also undermines the theoretical basis of regional *comparative advantage*, which was the philosophical lie used by Republicans for enacting the free trade policies.

Regional comparative advantage presumes regional boundaries and borders. The reason is that each region must have a different social welfare function, in order for Spain to derive an advantage in shipping wine to Great Britain.

As early as 1960, economists such as Stephen Hymer, were trying to place the intentional behavior of multinational corporate executives into a global theoretical framework. Hymer argued in *The International Operations of National Firms: a Study of Direct Foreign Investment*, that multinational corporations entered host states because the host states possessed certain assets that complimented the corporation's technological knowledge.

By entering a region to gain strategic knowledge, the corporation was able to gain property rights over future useful knowledge, gain rental payments on existing knowledge and politically influence the future direction of regional knowledge creation and diffusion, to benefit the interests of the multinational corporation.

One consequence of this trade policy tended to eliminate the supply chain of local exchange among American local firms.

Local commercial exchange in the American natural rights republic was one social force that tended to bind Americans to follow the rules that they give to themselves. In the natural rights republic, American society is held together by hundreds and thousands of commercial exchanges.

In a fair commercial exchange between social equals, no man can promote his own financial interest without promoting that of the other party to the exchange. The way Jefferson said this about social equality is that in the American natural rights republic "no man is so poor as to have to sell himself, and no man rich enough to be able to buy him."

This is the Jeffersonian idea that, under a natural rights constitution, we when we defend freedom for ourselves, we are compelled to defend the freedom of others.

In *The Lever of Riches*, Joel Mokyr reviews the relationship between economic development and technological innovation by first raising the question why economic growth occurs in some societies and not others.

Mokyr perceives an interplay of forces between social factors and economic factors that, in some cases, leads to technological innovation..

According to Mokyr, technological progress tends to occur in regional economies which have well-educated citizens, who are deeply engaged in the economic and political decisions of their communities.

In such a society, the creation of technical progress is rapidly diffused, and as the knowledge embodied in the change spreads among citizens, it creates imbalances and bottlenecks in existing inter-industry local exchange relations.

Mokyr analyzed the history of the Industrial Revolution to find clues about why it seemed to have such a favorable reception in England, and not in other countries. He speculated that in some countries there was "... a fear of loss suffered by established firms in industries being mechanized... which led to a type of political-economic sclerosis."

Mokyr noted, "Technological progress reduces the wealth of those possessing capital specific to the old technology that cannot be readily converted to the new."

At the beginning of the Industrial Revolution in Britain, the British ruling class had most of its capital assets in real estate and agriculture. According to Mokyr, "The politically dominant classes in Britain were the propertied classes, and technological innovation did not threaten to reduce the value of their assets."

In Mokyr's interpretation, it was the absence of opposition from the elite propertied classes in Britain, in comparison to the opposition of the elite in other European countries, which explained why the Industrial Revolution succeeded in Britain.

Technical change causes new income flows to be created where none had existed before. The ruling classes that perceive a threat to their income that results from technological innovation use the power of government to limit the effects.

The new interindustry relationships tend to create new sources of regional income that are not dependent on the older interindustry supply chain relationships.

Part of the new income is a result of increased productivity, meaning that output increases with reduced inputs in the production unit.

Part of the new income flows are a result of profits made in the new future markets.

And, as the case studied by Mokyr in Great Britain, sometimes it is the mere absence of organized political opposition to technical change that allows forces as powerful as those unleashed by the Industrial Revolution to take hold in a region.

From the financial perspective of global corporations, the threat of American individualistic technological innovation can be reduced if the corporations are the only units that control the rate and direction of innovation, by absorbing the innovation, inside their organizational framework.

If the corporations can control the pace and direction of technological innovation, then they will also be able to monopolize the future income resulting from new markets and incomes.

The political effect of corporate monopolization of future income is loss of freedom in the natural rights republic because it eliminates the possibility of upward occupational mobility that results from economic growth.

Technology is often defined as a body of knowledge about how things work. In "*Technical Change as Cultural Evolution,*" Richard Nelson states that "...technology needs to be understood as consisting of both a set of specific designs and practices, and a generic knowledge that surrounds these and provides an understanding of how things work, the key variables affecting performance, the nature of currently binding constraints and promising approaches to pushing these constraints back."

Nelson identifies the two key components of technology as the learning component and the knowledge component. Learning about technology generally occurs as a result of 3 social processes Nelson characterizes as:
- learning by doing,
- learning by using,
- interindustry learning, which is learning from commercial exchanges.

These processes of learning occur when suppliers, vendors, and customers share knowledge about technology. Each case of learning occurs within a regional network of social-business relationships, some of which occur on the floor of the production unit working with machines.

What happens in the process of learning is that mid-level managers, supervisors, technicians, scientists, engineers, technicians inside the production unit talk with each other every day about how things work, and they also talk with the service technicians, and supply vendors about binding constraints in the production process.

The pace of learning in the social network influences the quantity of technical knowledge that accumulates in a region. Consequently, the rate of knowledge creation depends on the intensity of local commercial exchanges between firms, in any given regional economy.

Some commercial exchange networks are more effective at generating knowledge than others. Abramovitz and David in *Convergence and Deferred Catch-Up: Productivity Leadership and the Waning American Exceptionalism*, made a special note of this important relationship between the pace of learning and the accumulation of knowledge, in America, prior to the enactment of the Republican trade policies.

They claim, "Insofar as the pace of learning depends on the accumulation of experience, it is influenced by the pace at which engineers and businessmen come into contact with new methods of production and with the capital goods in which they are embodied."

"Thus, the pace of technical advance," they write, "may depend on the portion of production activities that involves constructing and installing new capital equipment and related structures, as well as on the growth rate of the cumulative gross stocks that constitute the setting for learning by doing, and learning by using capital embodied technologies."

According to Rogers in *Diffusion of Innovations*, the "...communication channels, time and social structure, are the key components in the diffusion process."

In a local exchange economy, the new interindustry relationships are strengthened over time as individuals from the production units communicate with each other over how things work.

This is a cumulative feedback mechanism of technical change that contributes to the earlier feedback mechanism between the changing consumer preferences and the spending of incomes at the regional level between the two time periods.

Rather than an input-output supply chain relationship, Rogers defines technology in terms of a "cause and effect" relationship. For Rogers, "A technology is a design for instrumental action that reduces uncertainty in the cause-effect relationships involved in achieving a desired outcome."

Rogers acknowledges that technology is information, and that the transformation of information is a communication process. But, his specification of technology as a cause-effect relationship, presumes that technology always acts to reduce uncertainty.

In a natural rights republic, these mechanisms of knowledge diffusion are based upon local social exchange networks, and are not based upon price movements that are adjusting the economy to equilibrium, in the current time period.

As a result of the trade policies, local exchange economies were destroyed. Part of the reason for the government monetary policies, since 2002, that created the real estate asset bubbles, were due in part, to ameliorating the negative effects by using tax and fiscal policy for the parts of the regional economies that are not connected to global trade transactions.

The pace of technological innovation absorption was tested by Los and Verspagen in an input-output model that represented regional trading relationships.

In their work, *The Empirical Performance of A New Interindustry Technology Spillover Measure*, they developed a measure of "technological closeness" in production technology that was shared by firms in a distinct geographical region, defined by Wij.

Their measure of technological closeness in production technology is taken from a transaction matrix that develops the cosine between two column input vectors. By establishing the relationship between all pairs of sectors in a region, they were able to describe the extent of a common regional technological macrostructure.

One implication of their concept is that the greater the technological closeness of firms within a region, the greater the pace of technical change. So, in addition to causing a faster rate of technological absorption of an innovation, the pace of technological change in a local exchange economy would also increase.

As new production units in the regional industrial cluster adopted the newest innovation, the regional economy in the next time period two would be expected to show new supply chain trading relationships in the rows and columns of the input-output model used by Los and Verspagen.

The new and greater levels of interindustry coefficient linkages would be a result of new units buying and selling intermediate goods to each other.

The new markets created by technical change represent an entirely different economic structure, with its own internal dynamic of growth, than the production relationships in the former time period.

In the natural rights republic, characterized by open, competitive markets, the technological application of these mental insights occurs in the new regional entrepreneurial ventures created by the entrepreneurs.

American entrepreneurs, prior to 1992, relied upon the culture of freedom and the rule of law when they actualized and commercialized their ideas.

After the loss of freedom, resulting from the Republican trade policies, American entrepreneurs lost their most important competitive advantage to the large corporations, who had internalized the technological innovation process in each metro region across the world.

As a result of the Republican global trade policies, these types of mental images and insights, that commercialized innovation, occur almost exclusively inside the organizational structure of the global corporation.

Prior to 1992, the new ventures caused structural interindustry changes among the trading partners in a local supply chain of firms.

The region's pathway of technological innovation, prior to 1992, would have been determined by the technology that best served the as-yet developed future markets.

That sequence of economic events in upward mobility occurred as a matter of American history for about 230 years. The economic history of America has not been smooth, but at least under Madison's flawed arrangement, political establishments were stable.

After 1992, as a consequence of outsourcing innovation, the decisions to create new technology and new products became the exclusive province of the global corporations.

Wassily Leontief was raising this issue about the role of technological innovation in one of his last published papers in 1989, *Input-Output Data Base For Analysis of Technological Change*. He said, "Thus, the introduction of a new method of production in one sector cannot be adequately assessed without knowledge of changes taking place in the input-output structure of the other sectors."

Outsourcing American technology across global industrial sectors, after 2002, was made feasible by the deployment of ICT, and served to cut regional firms off from their traditional means of "knowing" about technical changes taking place in other sectors.

As pointed out by G. B. Richardson, global firms will internalize similar core competencies and externalize complementary activities through "collaborative relationships" with their outsourced regional producer firms in a geographical strategy that "...yields profits to the firms core competency."

As a result of the global trade policies, global corporations neither pay taxes to the national government that supports them, nor reinvest their profits in the nation that nurtured them.

They are citizens of the world, not citizens of America.

John Cantwell, in his article, *The Globalization of Technology: What Remains of the Product Cycle Model*, makes this same point about the global corporation's strategy of regional location related to the corporation's need-to know about technical change.

According to Cantwell, "In an integrated multinational corporate network, each affiliate specializes in accordance with the specific (input-output) needs of the corporation...characteristics of local production conditions technological capabilities and user requirements...in an attempt to exploit the technological potential of the location in which it is carried out....the MNC globalization and national (technical) specialization are complementary parts of a common process."

Franco Malerba and Luigi Orsenigo, in *Schumpeterian Patterns of Innovation*, discuss how regional "technological performance is strongly associated with the emergence of a stable group of innovators, who innovate consistently and continuously over time."

The regional economic stability in the rate of regional innovation is a result of a unique set of "...specialized skills, knowledge institutions, and resources that make up an underlying technological infrastructure" in the region.

If regional economies lose that knowledge base of specialized skills, then the regions lose the ability to generate economic growth. In other words, when all metro regions are the same, regions become dependent upon global corporations for creating jobs and incomes in their regions.

As the recent report by the Harvard Business School documents, job growth in America, since 2002, is concentrated in just 20 counties, that are corporate headquarters of global corporations.

Any single region in America has lost its comparative advantage of American ingenuity, and its ability for creating self-generated economic growth, based upon the region's unique skills and innovation capacity.

This development explains one of the reasons for the explosion of industrial recruitment incentives in states and regions. The elected representative at the local levels of government are dependent on global corporations for jobs, and must bribe them with tax dollars to locate a branch operation in their region.

After the recruitment of a branch global corporation, the control over the innovation in the region, the dynamic path of technical change of a region becomes dependent on the corporation's core competency.

The rate of offshoring innovation and American R&D increased after 1992, and increased dramatically again in 2002. One political problem for assessing this trend is that the agency responsible for collecting and reporting on this trend has stopped collecting data on the indicator.

Most of the offshoring related to the 1500 largest corporations legally domiciled in the United States has been targeted to their affiliate operations in India and China.

Diagram 3.1 Rate of Offshoring American R&D Innovation

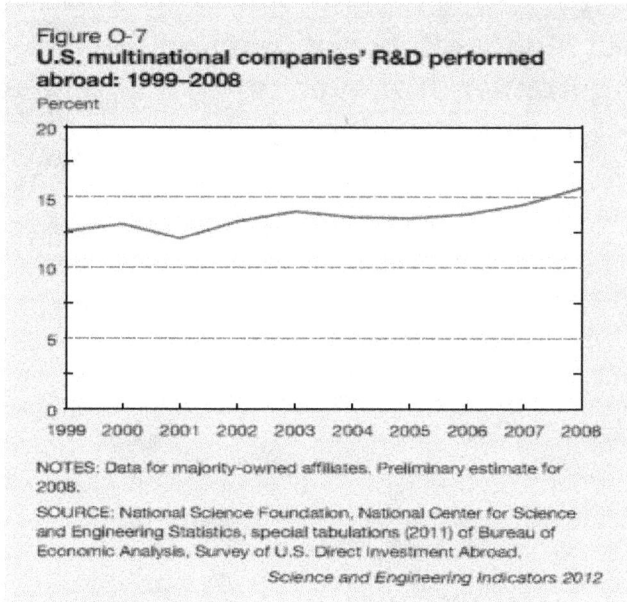
When large corporations offshore operations, there are two negative
economic effects on the domestic economy: There is an immediate loss of
manufacturing jobs in America, and then, later, there is a subsequent loss of
jobs as a result of the inability of the economy to innovate.

Global firms first established manufacturing facilities abroad (1985 – 1992).
Then, the global firms assigned increasingly complex products to the foreign
affiliates.

After about 5 years, the global corporations began locating R&D sites in close
proximity to the production and manufacturing factories.

These foreign R & D sites support the transfer of knowledge and prototypes
from the firm's home location to foreign manufacturing plants. The immediate
job losses are primarily in production occupations on the U. S. plant floor and
the subsequent job losses are in scientific, engineering and professional
occupations.

Research at Duke University indicates that upwards of 50% of the jobs in
Human Resources, Finance, Procurement and IT are immediately lost as a
result of offshoring.

When U.S. companies offshore their innovation functions to India, they do not
typically employ as many U.S. engineers or other scientific professionals in
the U.S. locations.

Diagram 3.2 Effect of Offshoring on Job Functions

IT remains the most highly offshored function. The next offshoring frontier, however, is globalizing product and process innovation

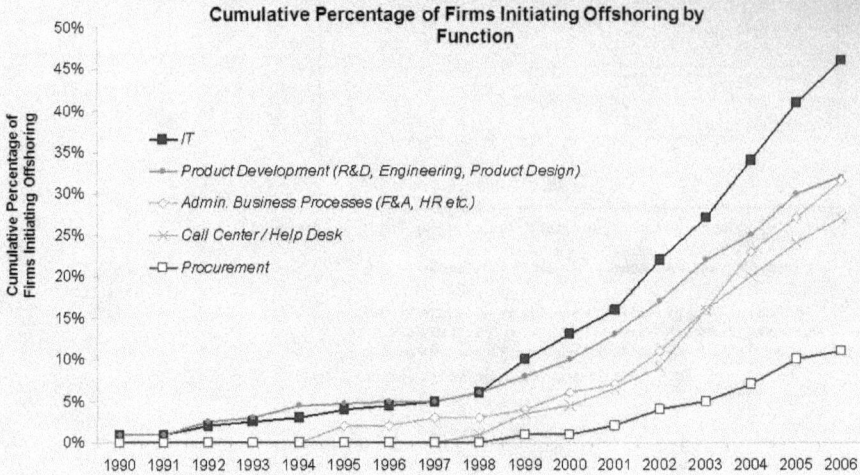

Cumulative Percentage of Firms Initiating Offshoring by Function

Y-axis: Cumulative Percentage of Firms Initiating Offshoring

Legend:
- ■ IT
- ◆ Product Development (R&D, Engineering, Product Design)
- ◇ Admin. Business Processes (F&A, HR etc.)
- ✕ Call Center / Help Desk
- □ Procurement

X-axis: 1990 1991 1992 1993 1994 1995 1996 1997 1998 1999 2000 2001 2002 2003 2004 2005 2006

Source: Duke University / Booz Allen Offshoring Research Network 2006 Survey

Diagram 3.3 Immediate Effect of Offshoring on Occupations

As Offshoring of Higher-Skilled Job Functions Grows, Fewer Jobs Are Likely to Be Lost in Advanced Economies

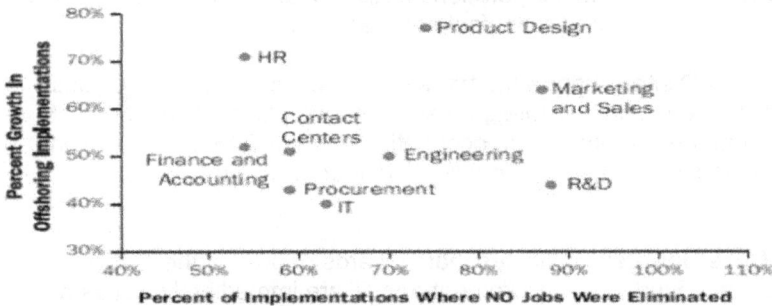

Y-axis: Percent Growth In Offshoring Implementations

Data points:
- Product Design
- HR
- Marketing and Sales
- Contact Centers
- Finance and Accounting
- Engineering
- Procurement
- R&D
- IT

X-axis: Percent of Implementations Where NO Jobs Were Eliminated (40% 50% 60% 70% 80% 90% 100% 110%)

Source: Duke University/Booz Allen Hamilton Offshoring Research Network 2006 Survey.

The large corporations buy their parts and supplies from global supply chains, not located in the
U. S. The loss of regional intermediate demand value chains in 350 metro regions is the single biggest economic structural change in the past 20 years.

Economists call this process regional "economic hollowing out."

Diagram 3.4 Loss of Intermediate Demand Value Chains Resulting From Offshoring

Component	Supplier	Company HQ Location	Estimated Factory Price	Price as % of total factory cost	Gross Profit Rate	Est'd Value Capture
Hard Drive	Toshiba	Japan	$73.39	50%	26.5%	$19.45
Display Module	Toshiba-Matsushita	Japan	$23.27	16%	28.7%	$6.85
Video/Multimedia Processor	Broadcom	US	$8.36	6%	52.5%	$4.39
Controller	PortalPlayer	US	$4.94	3%	44.8%	$2.21
Insertion, test, and assembly	Inventec	Taiwan	$3.70	2%	N.A.**	$3.70
Battery Pack	Unknown	Japan*	$2.89	2%	30%*	$0.87
Display Driver	Renesas	Japan	$2.88	2%	24.0%	$0.69
Mobile SDRAM Memory - 32 MB	Samsung	Korea	$2.37	2%	28.2%	$0.67
Back Enclosure	Unknown	Taiwan*	$2.30	2%	30%*	$0.69
Mainboard PCB	Unknown	Taiwan*	$1.90	1%	30%*	$0.57
Subtotal for 10 most expensive inputs			$126.00	85%		$36.96
All other inputs			$22.10	15%		
Total all iPod inputs			$148.10	100%		

Source: Portelligent, Inc., 2006 and authors' calculations
* Supposition based on other iPod models or Apple products
** See text for explanation of how Inventec's gross margin is calculated

When the Republicans abdicated freedom, they did so to benefit their global corporate special interests. Their political policies worked well for their special interests, as the representative case of Apple can describe.

Apple's profits have been very high during the recent U. S. economic collapse.

Diagram 3.5. Apple Inc. (AAPL) Profits

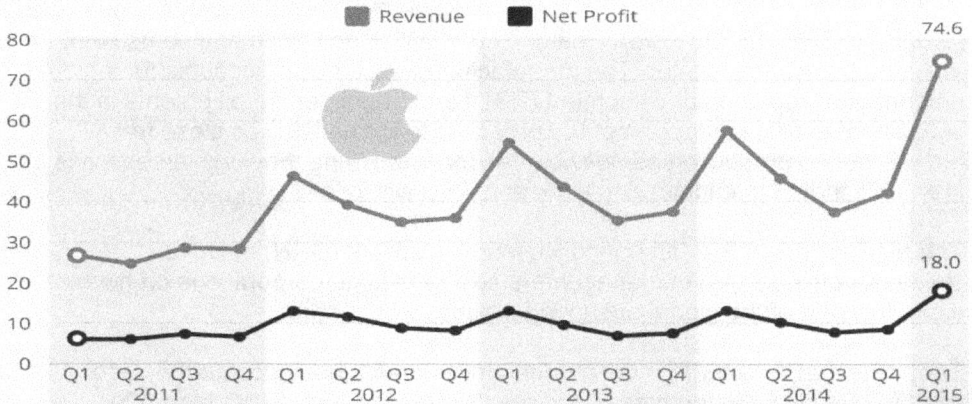

Apple's Historic Quarterly Earnings
Apple's revenue/net profit per business quarter (in billion U.S. dollars)

*Apple's business year ended on September 30th
Source: Apple

Forbes statista

47

While the tax and trade policies have destroyed much of the ability of the U. S. economy to innovate, the new global supply chain and global trade has been very profitable for companies like Apple and Cisco.

For example, for each Apple I Pod sold at a retail price of $299, Apple makes a net profit of $76.
Most of the rest of the net profit margin is made by Apple's foreign trading partners in the global supply chain.

Those profits used to be made, prior to 1992, in U. S. metro regional supply chains by small U. S. firms that supplied parts to Apple. As a result of the economic structural changes, most of jobs created in the U. S. from Apple's global production operations are in the nonprofessional low-paying retail positions.

Some economists call this the "Race to the Bottom."

Diagram 3.6 Wages and Salaries Related to Offshoring

	Production	Other non-professional	Engineering and other professional
U.S.	$47,640	$25,580	$85,000
Japan	$40,400	$20,000	$65,000
Korea	$29,440	$15,000	$50,000
Taiwan	$12,860	$7,000	$20,000
Singapore	$17,110	$9,000	$20,000
Philippines/Thailand	$2,140	$1,500	$15,000
China	$1,540	$1,000	$10,000

The average American job in the Apple iPod value chain for non-professional retail workers pays about $25,580. The average pay for engineering and other professional jobs is about $85,000.

The engineering and professional jobs are being shipped over to India.

As Hira and Hira (2005) note, "Nearly 41 percent of American engineers work in the manufacturing sector. The manufacturing sector also accounts for 62 percent of all research development (R&D) and 90 percent of all patents in the U.S. The prevailing management approach is to locate R&D as close to manufacturing production as possible. As manufacturing moves overseas, it is inevitable that both engineering work and R&D will follow."

The researchers at the Offshoring Research Network (ORN) at Duke University provide helpful management advice to large corporations on how to make this part of the global offshoring process work better.

They note that, "...after IT, new product development has become the second most frequently provided type of service. Small providers (fewer than 500 employees), in particular, specialize in offering product development functions from various locations around the world... Companies need to be prepared to rotate key people from domestic to offshore engineering and research facilities in order to monitor and ensure effective transfer of existing routines and institute necessary protocols for communication between the home and offshore teams."

The Duke University management consulting advice places special emphasis on the technique of "reverse knowledge transfer." They are describing how American knowledge can be more easily transferred from the United States to the foreign operations of the large corporations.

"Furthermore, as companies start to offshore higher end product development," they note, "either in-house (captive organization offshore) or outsourced to third-party providers, practices and routines for reverse knowledge transfer and flow need to be developed. For example, according to 2006 ORN survey results, some companies have experimented with hosting S&E staff from offshore locations to liaise and integrate with their counterparts in the home country."

There is an immediate direct loss of jobs, and then, later, a much bigger negative economic effect on the ability of the U. S. economy to innovate as a result of the metro regional value chains being destroyed.

Fifarek et al., used patent statistics to make their argument that the offshoring of innovation is destroying the nation's ability to innovate. Their research results suggest "that offshoring practices have adverse effects on innovation at the national home base."

"Using patent data as a measure of innovative performance in REE (rare earth technologies), we show that offshoring in material supply after 1990 is associated with a decline in the rate of US REE technology innovation. These results suggest a progressive loss of US REE technology innovation as elements of the innovation system are offshored. Informal conversations with one firm representative revealed that removing manufacturing from the US has also led to the removal of over 90% of domestic R&D activities on rare-earth permanent magnet materials. More importantly, the knowledge for producing NdFeB magnets within the US has been lost. US based manufacturers can no longer compete with the quality ofNdFeB magnets produced in China or Japan."

The extent of job loss in America was partially masked by an increase in service sector retail jobs. The importation of Apple products required an increased retail sales force. Not only do the retail jobs pay less, but as the case of Circuit City's recent liquidation demonstrates, the service industry jobs that are left behind are increasingly unstable.

Retail sales and consumer spending collapsed in America during the summer of 2008 when the speculative collusion in oil markets sucked the life out of consumer spending. The end of the oil speculation in October of 2008 did not come soon enough to save the jobs at Circuit City.

The trends in economic uncertainty are increasing among American citizens because they know something is wrong, but they cannot bring themselves to believe that their elected political leaders would deliberately sabotage the domestic economy in order to benefit the global corporations.

The political leaders lied to the American public about the consequences of the Republican trade policies, and the American voting population believed the lies that the new trade policies would be beneficial to the society, without the façade of the winners compensating the losers.

Diagram 3.7. Trends in Corporate Technology Sector Investment Since Offshoring Started

Real Nonresidential Fixed and Equipment & Software Investment

Percent change from year ago

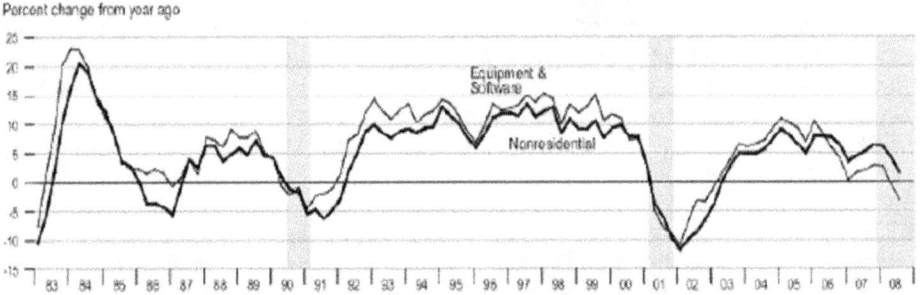

Corporate profits of U.S. corporations increased dramatically in 2002, after changes to U. S. trade and tax policies that encouraged U. S. corporations to make direct foreign investment (FDI). (AKA offshoring)

Diagram 3.8 Trends In Corporate Profit Rates Following Offshoring

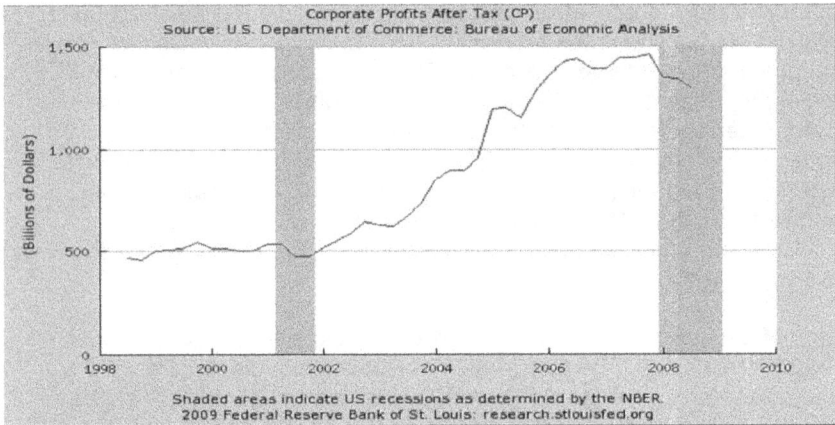

Corporate profits are going up as a result of global trade policies, promoted by the Republicans, but the rate of direct domestic investment in the U. S. economy is going down.

U. S. corporate profits made overseas are not being reinvested in the U. S. economy. Most of the investments and innovation activity for U. S. corporations is now taking place in India and China.

Diagram 3.9 Rate of Direct Domestic Investment Since Offshoring Started

Investment
Percent of nominal GDP

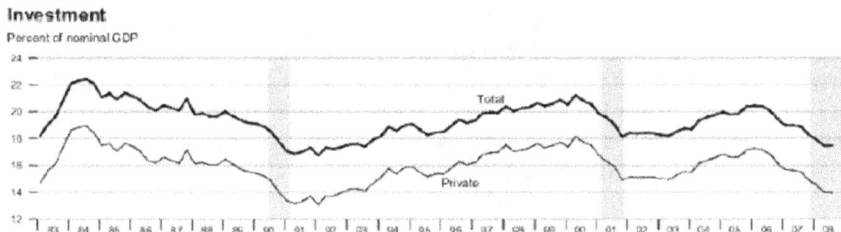

In addition to creating a structural labor market job deficit, the Republican policies eroded the 230-year tradition of Yankee ingenuity. This loss of technological innovation is more damaging, long term, to the economic viability of the American economy, than the structural damage to the labor market.

It was not simply the trade policies of 1992 and 2002 that ravaged the U. S. economy. Those laws were combined with research and scientific grants that skewed the financial benefits of university research into the coffers of the largest corporations. Prior to 2002, the U. S. Congress had implemented a number of laws aimed at boosting university research and technology transfer.

The laws passed by Congress in 1980 (The Bayh-Dole Act of 1980) to promote university research and development were intended to stimulate technology innovation and commercialization, that would lead to job creation. As the chart shows, the laws supported an enormous flow of both federal dollars and private corporate dollars, to universities, and provided a very lucrative business model, for the universities, to gain patent royalties from inventions made at the universities.

In their investigation into the financial effects of the Bayh-Dole Act, entitled, *The Impact of Private Ownership, Incentives and Local Development Objectives on University Technology Transfer Performance*, Sharon Belenzon and Mark Schankerman describe the most recent history, since the passage of the trade and tax laws. (CEP Discussion Paper No. 779, September 2007).

They note that, "Patenting and licensing by universities has grown sharply and has become an active public policy issue in the U.S. From 1991-2004, patent applications by U.S. universities rose from 1,584 to 10,517 and license income increased from $218 million to $1.4 billion, which is about six percent of federal R&D financing for universities. This rapid growth was partly associated with the Bayh-Dole Act of 1980, which gave universities ownership of inventions from federally-funded research."

The tech transfer process currently in operation at most American universities constitutes a closed loop system, where the knowledge created inside the university is fed directly into the global value chains, via the patent licensing process. That global knowledge never has a chance to enter the former regional value chains because those regional value chains do not exist, anymore.

51

Wendy Schacht, the congressional analyst cited above, is aware of this looming economic dilemma about knowledge creation and diffusion. As she notes in her report to Congress, "Thus, if the work performed in the academic environment is to be integrated into goods and services, (in the U. S. economy) a mechanism to link the two sectors (university and local industry) must be available. Prior to World War II, industry was the primary source of funding for basic research in universities. This financial support helped shape priorities and build relationships. However, after the war the federal government supplanted industry as the major financial contributor and became the principal determinant of the type and direction of the research performed in academic institutions. This situation resulted in a disconnect between the university and industrial communities."

She cites the recent statistics on how this process of joint university/large corporation tech transfer is working. "As of the end of 2007, 824 projects have been funded representing approximately $2.4 billion in federal financing matched by $2.2 billion in financing from the private sector. Of these projects, approximately 28% were or are joint ventures."

As Fifarek notes, this example, repeated hundreds of times across the country at multiple universities would have the consequence of undermining the national economic welfare based upon innovation. "Even if offshoring brings short-term economic benefits to the United States," they write, "in the form of gains to companies (increased profits) and consumers (lower prices), it could eventually undermine America's ability to innovate."

Kliesen, the economist for the Federal Reserve Bank, ends his article by noting that, "As an economic proposition, free trade benefits society because it has the potential to make all citizens better off without making any citizens worse off. In reality, while the benefits from trade are positive and sizable, (profits) international trade also produces losers (ordinary citizens). Chief among them are workers and owners of capital (shareholders) in industries that cannot compete with foreign manufacturers."

To summarize, large corporations can evade U. S. income taxes by never converting profits made overseas into U. S. currency, and can invest their profits in offshore R & D locations, while at the same time, they can obtain much lower tax rates on credits established for collaboration with U. S. universities. The trade laws create tax incentives for U. S. corporations to make investments overseas in foreign operations and to obtain tax credits from funds that they transfer to universities.

In 2008, when the time came to confront socialism, the Republicans opted, instead, to protect their special financial interests of the global corporations.

When Obama invokes his socialist class hatred invective that "it is George Bush's fault," what Obama and the socialists mean to say is that George Bush promoted the Republican political agenda on enacting economic policies, which subsequently destroyed the American comparative advantage in America's technological superiority.

The reason that the socialist propaganda resonates with 50% of American voters is that the socialist propaganda contains an element of truth about the Republicans.

Since 2000, the rate of new venture creation (new business birth rate) is less than half of the birth rate in the 1990s. The U. S. high-technology small businesses birth rate sharply increased in the mid-1990s, rising from around 1,000 annually to an annual average of about 1,400 from 1995 to 1999. It is now less than 500 per year.

This result is caused by the Republican abdication of freedom, which caused the decline in the birth rate of new ventures in America.

Diagram 4.1. Birth Rate of American New Technology Ventures Since 1992

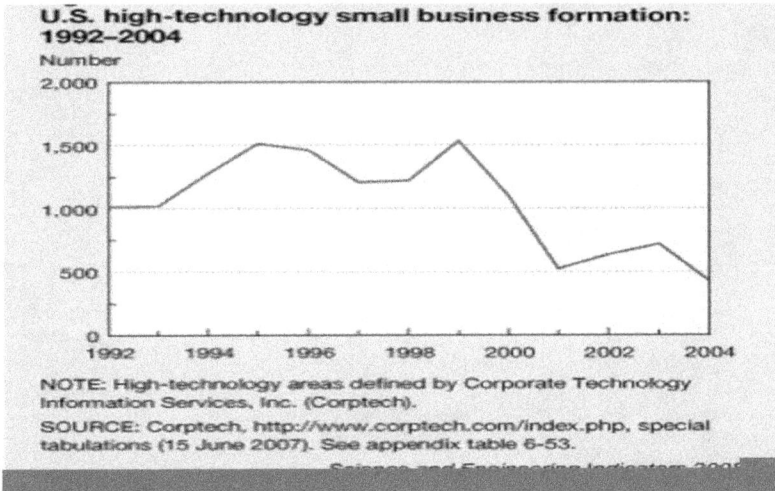

U.S. high-technology small business formation: 1992–2004

NOTE: High-technology areas defined by Corporate Technology Information Services, Inc. (Corptech).
SOURCE: Corptech, http://www.corptech.com/index.php, special tabulations (15 June 2007). See appendix table 6-53.

While the global corporations are making historically high profits, as a result of the new global trading patterns, their rate of direct domestic investment in innovation in America has declined.

Their profits are not being reinvested in American high technology sectors.

The most critical types of new business formation, in terms of job creation, are in nine high technology value chains. (Aka high tech). The economic reason for the importance of high tech investments is that those investments, in conventional economic theory, are "autonomous," meaning that the rate of investment is not subject to the dictates of government policy.

Prior to 1992, when these new firms were formed, they bought services and supplies from other U. S. small firms, in regional industrial value chains. The birth rate of these high tech firms has dropped dramatically since 2002, when the tax laws and trade policies were implemented. These firms were the job creation engine in the American economy.

That job creation engine has been shipped overseas to India and China. When the jobs were shipped overseas, the local interindustry value chains in local economies were eviscerated.

In a "*venture capital chicken/new venture creation egg*" dilemma, U. S. venture capital firms have abandoned investments in startups, beginning around 1999. The share of venture capital devoted to seed-startup financing peaked at 19% in 1994 and then declined precipitously, bottoming out just above 1% in 2002. The rate was 4% in 2006.

In a nation of 350 million citizens, and about 350,000 small private firms, there are only 500 deals done in the first quarter of 2016.

Most U. S. venture capital firms have established branch operations in India and China and are devoting profits made in capital gain exits from U. S. ventures to investments in foreign startups.

Diagram 4.2 Seed Stage Investing

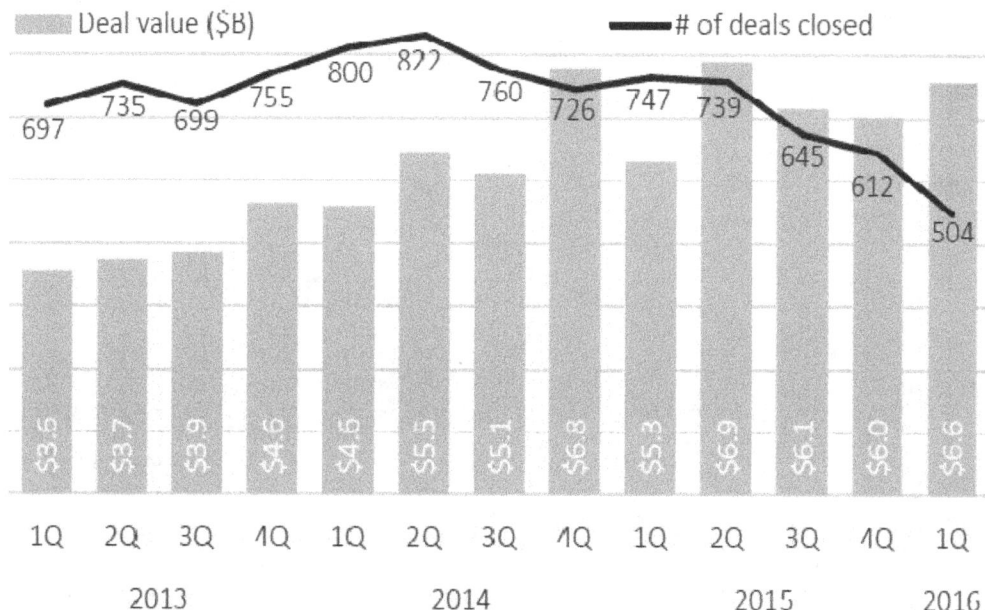

Source: PitchBook

At the same moment in American economic history that U. S. corporate profits are not being reinvested in the U. S. economy, the rate of angel capital and venture capital investments in domestic American firms is flat-lining.

Without investments, there is no economic growth. Without economic growth, there is no job growth. Without job growth, there is no upward occupational mobility. Without upward occupational mobility in a natural rights republic, common citizens turn to socialism.

While the overall rates of venture capital investments in the U. S. economy have dropped dramatically, the concentration of investments in just a handful of states means that the benefits from job creation in new ventures are not widely distributed across the nation's economy.

About 50% of the total VC investments occur in one state, California.

The structural economic weakness in the U.S. economy begins at the point where capital investment in small private firms, are not dispersed geographically, to 350 metro regional economies.

Diagram 4.3. Rate of Angel and Venture Capital Investing

A stratospheric rise in angel/seed activity has ended
U.S. VC activity (#) by stage and year

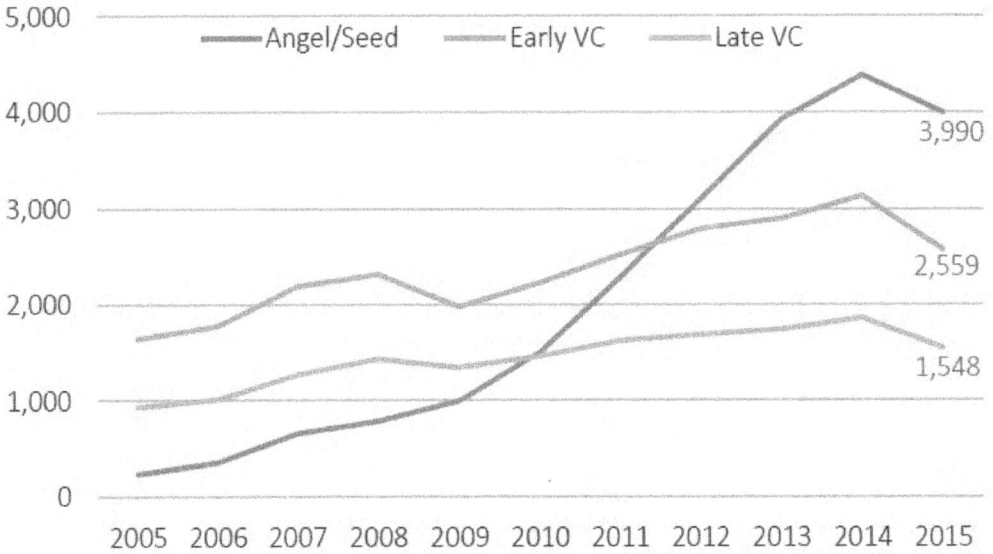

Source: PitchBook

Diagram 4.4. Venture Capital Investing By State

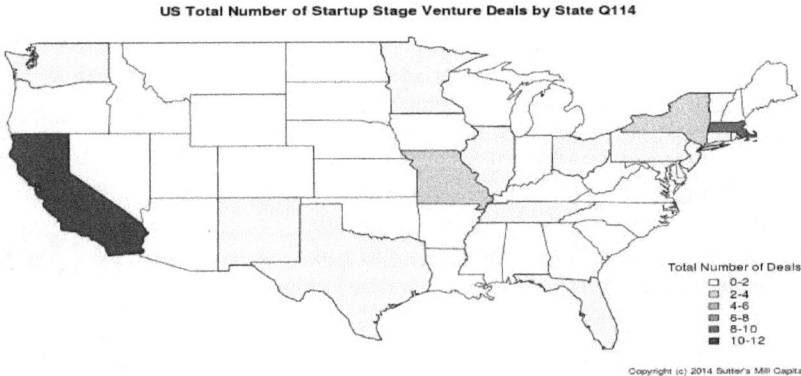

US Total Number of Startup Stage Venture Deals by State Q114

Total Number of Deals
0-2
2-4
4-6
6-8
8-10
10-12

Copyright (c) 2014 Sutter's Mill Capital

The capital investment in technology firms serves two important labor market functions.

First, within 3 years of the capital investment, a representative firm hires more workers. Prior to 2002, this part of the job market was the most important component of creating new jobs.

But, the capital investment performs an even more important function, in the long term, by creating new future markets, about 7 years after the period of investments. The future markets create new incomes and new wealth, for the next round of capital investments.

In other words, the new future markets distribute new wealth and incomes so that the income inequality is lower in a natural rights republic than in a global corporate economy, where income and wealth are concentrated in the hands of the few and the well borne.

The new future markets create future wealth. Without the opportunity to benefit from the future wealth creation, common citizens lose their faith in government that was supposed to protect their property.

Madison's flawed arrangement serves to benefit the few, at the expense of the many.

When the Republicans failed to defend freedom from the socialist transformation, one consequence of their abdication was the destruction of the ability of the American economy to have a high rate of new venture creation.

Professor Ed Feser, of the University of Illinois, modified the conventional input-output transaction table to describe how the nine high technology value chains in America have been affected by recent economic events. (*Globalization, Regional Economic Policy and Research*, 2005).

As the research below indicates, each of the nine high technology value chains in America is experiencing job loss. Beyond the recent immediate job losses at the national aggregate level, there is a more fundamental negative economic effect being described by the Feser research.

The job loss in the most important technology value chains reflects the destruction of the regional industrial value chains in each metro regional economy.

When the regional value chains are removed, via offshoring, the opportunities for investment in new ventures in those regional economies also disappear. Offshoring innovation has had the effect of removing the most important economic component of the innovation-capital market investment mechanism that used to exist in America.

Fifarek et al., place special emphasis on the transactions that occur among members of the regional value chains in his research on innovation. As they note, "results have shown that the innovation trajectory of an industry can be strongly conditioned by the role of upstream suppliers of materials and production equipment, and even those associated with their research equipment (Levin et al., 1987; Klevorick et al., 1995; Linder et al., 2005; Chapman and Corso, 2005). Likewise, innovation can also be affected by downstream entities, including professional and technical societies, independent inventors, and users of the industry's product (Levin et al., 1987; Hippel, 1988; Linder et al., 2005; Chapman and Corso, 2005).

Fifarek notes, "that removal of any one of these organizations (in the innovation system) may affect the innovation production within the system boundary. Such removal may be a direct result of the offshoring, such as a decision to locate or outsource research and development activities abroad, outside a national system boundary. It may also be an indirect result of removing knowledge, by offshoring manufacturing operations or services, thus separating relationships, and reducing technology interests within the system boundary. In fact, upstream suppliers and downstream users are critical sources of knowledge for technical advances of a set of firms, and often more important than established sources of knowledge such as universities or government laboratories (Klevorick et al., 1995; Council on Competitiveness, 2005)."

In their finely granular analysis of how this offshoring of innovation affects America's regional value chains, Greg Linden, Jason Dedrick and Kenneth L. Kraemer describe the production and sale of the Apple iPod (*Innovation and Job Creation in a Global Economy: The Case of Apple's iPod*, January 2009).

"As recently as 2000," they note, "over one-third of the jobs in the U.S. computer industry were production jobs. By 2007, the number of production workers had fallen to less than one-sixth of total employment, and total production jobs had been cut in half just since 2002 (Figure 1). At the same time, white collar employment in the U.S computer industry was falling much more slowly, by about 10% in total from 2002 to 2007."

Linden et al., describe how the global value chains in the production of the iPod have replaced the U. S. regional value chains. They state, "But if globalization leads to a hollowing out of professional jobs as well as manufacturing, then innovation will only benefit shareholders, consumers, and a small number of top managers and professionals in the U.S."

The economic effect of offshoring is that America's ability to innovate in the 350 metro regional value chains has been hollowed out. The most important foundation for innovation in America was the small manufacturing firms in America, and about ½ of those firms no longer exist because the regional industrial value chains no longer exist in America.

Prior to 2002, this important component of the American innovation system created and diffused knowledge and served to distribute the employment and income multipliers. As a result of offshoring, the American foundation of innovation in the regional value chains that used to exist in the metro regions now exist in India and China.

When the Republicans abdicated their responsibility to defend freedom, one consequence was to eliminate the regional economic relationships among small firms in metro regions. Those relationships are commonly called supply chains, and they served a dual purpose of creating jobs in metro regions, and diffusing technological knowledge.

The technological innovation that previously occurred in metro regions was shifted to internal corporate supply chains, so that the benefits of innovation stayed within the corporation.

The Republicans protected the financial welfare of their special interests, to the detriment of citizens in the metro regions, when they abandoned freedom.

Regional economic growth is a process that occurs as a result of diversification of products and industrial sectors in a metropolitan area. The diversification is caused by technical change in production processes, which increase productivity. The improved productivity creates new flows of income, and creates new pools of venture capital, which can potentially be invested in a second generation of new ventures.

In his most recent work, "*Innovation, Knowledge Creation and Systems of Innovation,*" Manfred Fischer compared and contrasted the two trends in regional growth regarding technical change that occur simultaneously.

One trend identified by Fischer involves "the process of globalization of factor and commodity markets." The other trend involves the "regionalisation of knowledge creation and learning." These two trends are not entirely compatible, and lead to certain types of conflicts of interest.

The trends toward globalization and further development of the global corporate macrostructure of technology are compatible and supported by a political framework of global corporate special interests. These special interests meet and mingle every year, by invitation only, in Davos, with the elected representatives of host regions and nations.

When the executives of the global corporations meet elected political representatives in Davos, they discuss how all of them can stabilize their fluctuating global revenue streams through a number of strategies, some of which include the strategic location of parts of the global operations in carefully selected regional metro markets.

Davos is only the most visible of hundreds of social networking events that occur every day among corporate executives and national leaders.

The logic of the location decision will involve how best to fill the corporation's need for technical change in both production processes and new product development that are related to protecting the corporation's core technical competency. The decision will be framed against the backdrop of rapidly changing product life-cycles in fast moving global markets.

All of the executives share a common interest in a stable global market, even though they may compete in various forms of products and technology.

Zoltan Acs has described this global corporate location decision as a competitive strategy for obtaining both the local market share and the local technology of the indigenous firms.

As he points out in *Regional Innovation, Knowledge and Global Change*, indigenous firms have an early advantage over the global firms in terms of "the local environment and already have established relationships with vertically related businesses ranging from intermediate suppliers to local governments to local consumers... Multinational corporations must locate design and production facilities in these metro areas to overcome local indigenous firms home-court advantage."

The global corporation's need for seeking out certain regions as a resource base to enhance the core technical competency is different than the region's reliance on technical change as a progenitor of economic growth. Both the global corporations and the regional economy, rely on technical change to accomplish certain goals. They both need technological innovation, but for different reasons.

Their relationship, for this reason, is non-symmetrical, in the sense that the goals and needs are different, but also because the corporation's behavior can be modeled with a defined objective function and with an identifiable set of actors who direct the corporation's behavior towards the fulfillment of those objectives.

On the other hand, the regional economic or financial ends vary according to the set of political rules and political parties who share power, at any moment in time. Part of this issue of end goals for regional economies is that the U. S. constitution fails to define, and state, unambiguously, that the freedom of individuals to pursue their own freedom and welfare is the end goal of the government.

By locating in a specific region that is experiencing rapid technical change in production processes, the corporation is seeking to gain knowledge to stabilize the uncertain global market conditions. The ultimate goal is to redirect and internalize the regional economic technological trajectory to serve the needs of the multinational corporation.

According to Christoforo Bertuglia, et al., in, *An Interpretive Survey of Innovative Behavior and Diffusion*, a detailed analysis of these relationships provides the "...most uncertainty-reducing factors... a set of territorial relationships encompassing in a coherent way, a production system...which generates a dynamic collective learning process."

It is a result of being a producing member of the regional intermediate demand, input-output relationships, that exist in certain regions, that the senior managers in a global corporation "learn" about technical change as it relates to the corporation's core competency.

Over time, the multinational corporation's technological influence on the regional economy becomes greater than the influence formerly exerted by the local indigenous industrial cluster of firms.

James Utterback has described this influence as the "dominant design" influence. In *Mastering the Dynamics of Innovation: How Companies Can Seize Opportunities In the Face of Technological Change*, he states the sequence of events this way, "As the market grows, greater emphasis will usually be given to development of components tailored especially for the product itself... leading to a dominant design... Once a (dominant) design is accepted, it can have a profound impact both in the direction and the rate of further technical advance and on the structure of competition."

The second reason why global corporations seek to locate parts of their operations in certain regional markets concerns the need for corporations to use public resources and local economic resources to benefit the global corporate strategy. While the first reason has more to do with gaining knowledge about technological changes in the existing production technology process, this second reason has more to do with production improvements and product innovation related to global market forces that cause rapid product cycles.

The public resources, such as tax incentives, are used by the corporation to drop their costs of production, and to shift the risk of global technological obsolescence from themselves to the regional governments. Because each regional economy has a unique history and path of technical change, some of which complements the competency of the global corporation, the corporation will seek certain regions in order to absorb "spillovers" from the unique labor market skills and economic assets of the region.

Alan Southern, in *The Political Salience of The Space Flows*, described how the UK government used public resources to attract a Nissan auto plant to Sunderland. The goal was to use public resources to attract "inward investments" from global corporations. As he noted, "...the arrival of Nissan on the outskirts of the city in the 1980's established a new set of manufacturing principles in the area."

The irony of this example in the use of public resources is that it set up the conditions for repeating the regional weakness of the prior regional economy in the next time period. As Southern noted, the prior economic base of the region was in shipbuilding and coal mining, both of which had become obsolete as a result of global trade.

The new strategy of inward global corporate investment makes the regional economy even more dependent and vulnerable to global trade without extracting any concomitant long-term benefits to the workers in the region. The workers in the region had undergone publicly financed training to provide Nissan with "a workforce with the skills to match the requirements of new-telematic related industries."

As soon as global conditions required a change, Nissan could easily move the manufacturing operations to some other low wage region of the world.

In *Production Processes and Technical Change*, Morroni described a common phenomena in high economic growth regions. He found "... a constellation of firms with a leading firm and a cluster of complementary organizations, or a network of independent firms with collaborative relationships... these collaborative co-operative linkages enable certain economies of scale to be achieved through high overall production volumes."

To the extent that the metro region has a high rate, or pace of technical learning, and has citizens who have accumulated technical knowledge, it will have a high rate of technical change in production processes, and consequently, a high rate of economic growth. To the extent that ambient cultural values embrace individual freedom and entrepreneurial risk-taking, the region will have a high rate of new venture creation.

The concept of a geographically specific technological cluster of industries, characterized by a regional macrostructure, is important for defining the conflict of interest between global corporations and regional elected representatives. Under one arrangement, local firms form networks of relationships in the regional cluster that benefits the technological absorption of technical change in a production process.

Under another type of political arrangement, for example when local elected Republicans cooperate with national Republicans on issues like industrial recruitment tax incentives and global trade policies, the relationships of firms in the region tend to serve the interests of the global corporations.

Absorption and diffusion of technology within the macrostructure occurs as a result of a new production technique being adopted by many firms as a result of competitive imitation. All of the engineers, scientists, mid-level managers in the region communicate with each other about how the new process is working, and when and if they leave to create their own new venture, it is that new process that forms the basis on their own equipment and machinery purchases.

The conflict of interest between multinational corporations and regions involve both control over technological innovation, and the power to control when, where, and how the profits from technological innovation are used.

The reinvestment of profits, or what Schumpeter calls "entrepreneurial profits," does not depend on cash flow from old production units, nor is it related to the conventional loans made by commercial bankers, in what Schumpeter calls the static circular flow of existing firms.

Under one set of conditions involving how profits are re-invested, the result would possibly be self-sustaining regional growth in native firms. That possible outcome is contingent on a number of independent events lining up and occurring in a logical sequence in one time period, and then, by chance, meeting a favorable set of circumstances in a future time period.

Under another set of conditions, regional economic dependency is created when global corporations control both knowledge flows and profit reinvestment in the regional economy in the first time period in order that they gain some control over uncertain outcomes in the second time period.

The increased information flows related to technological innovation are related to increased production flexibility on a global scale, as Nathan Rosenberg pointed out, the "development of complementary strategic and cooperative relations with other firms. Through a telematic network, a firm can acquire its semi-finished goods and production services, and thus enrich its productions mix."

This increased flexibility is facilitated by the trends toward automated production techniques and computer information flows, which tends to increase the rate of regional technical change that benefits the corporation's core technological competency.

As discussed above, Coombs and Saviotti state that innovating firms are not uniformly distributed across geographical territory. Innovative firms tend to be located near other innovative firms. This tendency of innovating firms to concentrate in a region contributes to the development of a regional economic production macrotechnology.

The reason one region develops a macrotechnology as opposed to any other region, Coombs and Saviotti note, is related to the "...specific institutional configurations and by the cumulative, local, and specific character of the knowledge that the institutions possess." Institutional configurations include the variables of cultural values, especially as they relate to acts of individual entrepreneurs.

Some cultural values support the individual freedom to create new ventures, and some cultural values do not. One consequence of the Republican abdication of freedom is that it destroyed the cultural values of freedom by allowing the socialist values to replace them, and eliminated the incentives of regional entrepreneurs to obtain their future rewards.

Saviotti notes that innovative firms "...tend to cluster in those (areas) that were already innovating countries (or regions)... this specificity can not be explained by factor endowments, but is more likely to be caused by specific institutional configurations, and by the cumulative, local and specific character of the knowledge that the institutions possess."

For technological progress to occur, according to Mokyr, "...it must be born into a socially sympathetic environment." A sympathetic environment involves the values of trust and morality in economic relationships. In other words, it depends on adherence to the rule of law, in a free society, that allows individuals to reap future rewards, not taken away in high taxes or other confiscatory schemes imposed by the socialists.

Granovetter discusses this concept in terms of a "moral economy" for the social/business network within a region. The moral economy is the degree to which a business network is based upon trustworthy behavior, and mutual expectations of reciprocity. The trust and mutual expectations are geographically-bounded and encompass a loyalty to the wealth of the region, as contrasted with the corporate allegiance to global corporate governance.

In a region with a moral economy, certain non-contractual deals can be undertaken without suspicion of exploitation. This ability to trust another person in an uncertain economic environment, where neither party has full knowledge of exactly how the new production technology will actually function, once it is implemented on the plant floor, is important for obtaining future profits from the intellectual technological property.

In "*Technological Systems and Economic Development Potential: Four Swedish Case Studies*," Bo Carlsson described how a business social network opposed to technical change could influence a much wider social network of organizations. He described the case where "...there may be a certain self-reinforcing mechanism at work... A vicious circle, in which (existing) industry chooses not to become involved in an expanding technology, influencing universities and government policy makers to make the same choice."

E. J. Feser, in "*Old and New Theories of Industry Clusters*," makes this same point about the relationship between the global technical macrostructure and regional technical change. "One can also conceive of market power among some cluster members as exerting a detrimental influence on the overall cluster. For example, short-term, least-cost-focused contracting practices of OEMs with their suppliers may actually discourage strategic thinking and investments."

The important point in understanding the conflict of interest between global corporations and regions is to distinguish the type of technological innovation the region achieves under the influence of the global corporations located within the region. The type and extent of the regional technical change is different than what the region would have experienced in the absence of the influence by multinational corporations on the region's pathway of technical change.

The presence of the influence of the global corporation tends to skew the region's pathway towards serving the needs of the global corporation and tends to skew the types of business/social networks that form in the region to serving the political special interests of the corporation.

This is the outcome sought by the Republican Party through the adoption of the trade policies of 1992 and 2002.

The type of global corporate business-social network at the regional level, described by Carlsson, often is connected to a much larger network at the national and international level. The communication connection is via the new ICT. When the world's corporate elite meet each year in Davos, they are coordinating how the global market will function to meet their own corporate needs.

As described by Rod Coombs, in *Economics and Technical Change*, across all industrially advanced regions in the world in the largest global corporations, there is a trend towards convergence of industrial production techniques. Whatever industrial process occurs on the floor of a production unit in Malaysia can easily be replicated on a production floor in North Carolina.

As he states, "A major consequence of this analysis is that technological opportunities are to some extent... common to some groups of firms. This suggests that there will be some structure to the pattern of innovations generated at the industry level... Natural trajectories and various kinds of technological paradigms evolve in the course of time. Common patterns of technological economic behavior are gradually adopted by different firms even when they start from different initial trajectories."

This common technology of a global macrostructure is different than the regional economic macrostructure. Following the thesis of Schumpeter, multinational corporations have a different private interest in the global macrostructure of technology than the public purpose interest that an elected leader may have in promoting regional economic development through maximum rates of technological innovation.

Future regional economic development, based upon self-sustaining economic growth, will depend to a maximum extent on the creation of new ventures by entrepreneurs who act as the agents of technical change, and not on the global macro-technological innovations, whose benefits are internalized primarily by global corporations.

The strength of each region in escaping from the trends towards a global macrostructure lies both in the ability to extend the path of historical specialization in each regional economy and in the maintaining the ambient cultural values about entrepreneurship and individual freedom.

This question concerns the political control and accountability over trends in technology, and how technical change is related to the public purpose of individual freedom. The nature of the conflict of interests between global corporations and regions is over who absorbs the benefits of technical innovations.

The pace of technical absorption generates a cumulative feedback mechanism that influences the path of economic development in the region, via what Rostow has called the "plowback of profits for plant and equipment."

It is not plowback from net positive cash flow from operations, but entrepreneurial profits generated from either capital gains on venture capital investments, or as a result of the merger and acquisition of the new ventures by other corporations. The profits from the capital gain events are commonly called the "exit event."

Schumpeter was concerned that if commercial bankers formed a political alliance with monopoly corporations, the flow of investment capital to new ventures would be limited. Good new ventures would not get the investment capital they needed because of the banker's financial concerns with loan repayment from the old production units.

In other words, the banker has a conflict of financial interest that involves a preference for old production units over new units. From the perspective of the banker, the type of small flexible production unit preferred by the entrepreneur would not be the type of production unit favored by the banker. The banker's decision can influences the pace of technical change at the regional level.

Schumpeter wrote about the role of "inherited capital" played in the investment process, and cited commercial bankers as the intermediaries who used the inherited capital for investments in entrepreneurial ventures. It seems like his use of the term "inherited capital" is more like the description of venture capital than loanable funds.

But, in his description of what commercial bankers did with the inherited capital, Schumpeter emphasized the commercial loan aspects of new venture creation, and not equity investments.

In Schumpeter's model, commercial bankers "...supplied the entrepreneurs with purchasing power" by furnishing them with credit. Moreover, because bankers are not able to create credit in unlimited quantities, they have to select from among the investment plans put forward by entrepreneurs that they regarded as most desirable or likely to succeed.

Because of this decision-making power over credit, the direction of the pathway that the economy will follow will depend on the investment plans that are chosen, and therefore, it is bankers in Schumpeter's model who constitute the selection committees for investment plans. Schumpeter called the bankers the "helmsmen of the capitalist economy."

However, the commercial bankers of the 1920's described by Schumpeter are not necessarily the helmsmen of the regional economy today unless the direction of the economy favors the status quo of loan repayments to banks. Bankers are risk averse, and depend on continuing flows of cash from old production units for loan repayments. Their aversion to risk and their dependency on an existing stock of capital to generate cash flow depends on consumer preferences remaining stable.

Technical change causes consumer preferences to change, which would jeopardize loan repayments. If bankers are helmsmen, they are the kind who avoids the creative gales of destruction caused by technical change.

Hyman Minsky updates Schumpeter's concern with his analysis of global managed corporate capitalism. Managed global corporate capitalism is what happens every year in Davos.

In *Schumpeter: Finance and Evolution*, Minsky states that under the conditions of managed capitalism, the big pension funds, mutual funds, trust funds, otherwise known as institutional money, require cash flow in the near term to support the stock prices and their heavy levels of indebtedness on liability structures that they have securitized.

The emphasis on short term cash flow is somewhat at odds with the longer term investment horizons of the executives of global corporations, who are dealing with uncertain future global markets. In the case of institutional money for short-term cash flow, if the global corporations form a political alliance with the financial institutions to favor the status quo, the rate of regional technical change will be negatively affected.

The financial conflict of interest in this alliance is between the liquidity needs of the global financial institutions who depend on an indivisible stock of capital for cash flow, and the longer-term financial interests of global corporations. In Davos, the global banking and financial system is coordinated with the needs of the global corporations to smooth out the uncertainty in global markets.

Charles Kindleberger, in *World Economic Primacy*, noted how a certain set of national cultural values tended to favor an attitude towards technical innovation. He characterized this attitude as the "...capability and will of individuals, companies and governments to break free of existing habits, perceptions, institutions, and task allocations, in order to revise them in light of constantly changing circumstances and developments."

The strength of each region in escaping from the trends towards the total global politicalization of decisions involving technological innovation lies in the path of historical diversity of firms and skills of the labor force in each regional economy. It is the historical diversity of each region's economy that, under the favorable set of institutional arrangements, can promote the highest rates of technical change.

The goals of the multinational corporation in reaping monopoly profits through increasing scale of production are not compatible or consistent with the regional goal of self-sustaining economic growth caused by technical change.

Corporations have a financial interest in maintaining the status quo position of power by electing Republicans who are sympathetic to their financial goals. Corporations want to protect private/proprietary flows of technical information in order to absorb, internally, as much benefit from technology as possible. Maximum rates of technical knowledge diffusion, on the other hand, would require open, public flows of technical information.

Private, proprietary control of information is becoming much more important to corporations as a result of the new information communication technology. Global corporations are having a difficult time defining the boundaries of their corporate property rights to appropriate profits from intellectual property as a result of outsourcing most of their production processes. It is therefore, in their best interests to control and restrict the flow of information to enhancing the corporation's own core technical competency.

Global corporations would want to restrict the flow of key personnel from moving from the firm and taking technical knowledge with them to create new ventures. However, promotion of regional technical change involves the creation of hundreds of new ventures in multiple industrial sectors. The entrepreneurs for the new ventures are generally drawn from the ranks of existing large corporations.

In their criticisms of Clayton Christensen's work on disruptive innovations, one of the arguments made by Walsh and Kirchhoff, in *Entrepreneurs' Opportunities In Technology Based Markets* was Christensen's initial assumption about the price and quality of a new product. Christensen advises multinational firms to create small subsidiary firms to handle the task of product innovation. But Christensens' advice is based upon an incorrect assumption that new disruptive technologies have higher costs and poorer performance than existing products.

As noted by Walsh and Kirchhoff, "Small units of established firms undoubtedly will experience pressures to meet the needs of the existing customer base and technological mainstream of the parent firms. In this way, they will be inclined to look for new products or replacement products to fit existing markets. This focus will inhibit their efforts to develop the creative destroying innovations that could make a major impact."

A regional economy that had been following a certain pathway of technical change and had built up some historical regional advantages in innovation from local small firms in other regions would have a greater chance at economic growth than regions that had relied on the small firms of the multinational corporations. The regional advantage is based upon product diversity that is caused by technological variety that cannot be easily replicated in other regions.

For example, prior to 1992, the comparative national advantage in America made it difficult for more socialistic societies to replicate the technology innovation capacity of American entrepreneurs.

In some cases, these regional advantages in product diversity created by small local firms are very compelling as resources for serving the needs of corporations. Through political influence, the corporations seek to redirect the technological trajectory of the region to serve the needs of the corporation.

In the regional setting, under one set of cultural/political values that are oriented to maximum individual freedom and occupational mobility, the type of government policies pursued would include removing competitive barriers to entry in occupations, and impediments to the creation of new ventures, and the facilitation of open communication channels for the maximum diffusion of technical knowledge in extensive social-business networks.

Under a different set of cultural/political values, elected leaders would favor policies that were oriented to serving the needs of multinational corporation, with the type of trade policies and monetary policies pursued by the Republicans since 1992.

As a result of the restructuring, downsizing, and layoffs of middle management in America, the global corporations have cut themselves off from the traditional way of gaining new knowledge from "thinking and doing" as it relates to predicting the direction of technology.

According to Best, the global corporation will make up for this thinking and doing gap, by "...creating horizontal information flows across functional boundaries inside firms, and flows across industrial sectors by locating certain components of global operations in strategically selected regions."

This is the pathway chosen by Nissan when it located a part of its branch operations in Sunderland. It obtained the dual benefits of a public subsidy in production, and absorbed the technological knowledge that could be gained from the skilled labor force in the region. The local elected officials delivered the skilled labor force on a silver platter to Nissan.

The third reason why a region with a certain configuration of technology will become more important to global corporations than other regions concerns the relatively new phenomenon of making money from the sale of internally created new ventures and other types of spin-offs.

The subsidiaries are created as a part of the corporation's protection of its core competency. Certain regions have a history of technology that is compatible with the corporation's technical competency, and thus act as a likely target market for the sale of the subsidiaries. If the new technology is not lucrative enough, or does not exactly fit with the future direction of the corporation, the best strategy is to sell the technology as a functioning commercial organization.

J. B. Goddard, in *The Impact of New Information Technology on Urban and Regional Structure in Europe*, has described how difficult it is for a corporation to maintain global technical leadership over time. Facing uncertainty over the continued viability of the corporation's core technological competency, and cut off from traditional sources of "new" knowledge, the corporation will seek locations in regions experiencing rapid technical change.

Within those regions, the corporation will make venture capital investments in new ventures that may not be directly related to the core technical competency, but that could evolve onto a pathway that would eventually affect the core competency. By having an early ownership interest in the new ventures, the global corporation can gain new knowledge, while influencing the direction of the regional technology in new ventures to complement the corporation's core competency.

Plus, the corporation also obtains a new source of revenue from capital gains, when and if it either sells its ownership interest in the "exit" event or the new venture is merged or acquired, as would be the goal of any venture capitalist.

Goddard and Richardson described this third reason why global corporations will seek to locate in certain regions. A certain geographical location is a response by corporations to derive revenues from "service after the sale" in the new e-global commerce market place.

"What is not in doubt," they say in *Why Geography Will Still Matter: What Jobs Go Where*, is that the most significant employment effects are arising in the area of direct services to the consumer. Here the traditional close geographical (retail shop) relationship between the customer and supplier (in the global telematic network) of service is breaking down."

As a replacement for the prior multiple local independent retail service establishments, the corporation locates a branch service facility in a metro region to absorb revenues related to servicing the products.

Bell and Pavitt have pointed out that the resources that global corporations "need" from regional technical change may not be exactly the same resources a region "needs" from technical change in order to facilitate new venture creation.

As cited in *Globalization, Information Technology and Development*, they distinguish indigenous technological capabilities with the technological core competency of corporations. They cite three mechanisms at work as being essential for facilitating regional technical change:
- Inter-firm migration of skilled personnel who possess knowledge of new areas of technology.
- Infrastructure institutions, like think tanks, and research universities that assist in the process of innovation and absorption,
- and the education and skill training that occurs in firms, especially in the areas of product and process engineering.

Diagram 5.1 summarizes the reasons why global corporations will seek strategic locations in certain metropolitan regions.

Diagram 5.1. Why Corporations Locate In Regions

Corporations need regional resources->	Corporate Location Strategy
Need to know about production process technology	Will outsource production processes to regions with regional technology most compatible to core competency
Need to know about new product technology	Will form partnerships in regions with intermediate demand sectors experiencing rapid technical change
Need to create and spinoff new venture subsidiaries related to core competency	Will seek regions with stable group of industrial innovators related to core competency
Need new knowledge to supplement R & D in core competency	Will seek venture capital investments in new ventures in regions with tangential technical change
Need markets to sell products	Will seek regions with rapid technical change

Complementary technological competence between the technology of the corporation that is imported into the region, and the pathway of local technological accumulation in the region, which leads to a process of reciprocal technology transfer.

These regional mechanisms sometimes conflict with the needs of the global corporation, given a certain type of regional economic development welfare function. Regional economic development occurs as a result of technical change in production units, generally, manufacturing plants.

One of the important causal relationships that change as a result of technical progress is the one between incomes and consumer preferences for Pasinetti explains, in *Structural Change and Economic Growth: A Theoretical Essay On The Dynamics of The Wealth of Nations,* that the entrepreneur is faced with a choice of technique at the moment of plant design.

Simon Kuznets described the main conceptual relationships between technical change and economic growth in his 1930 book, *Secular Movements In Production and Prices.* Using the framework of a three-period cycle of time, Kuznets described how, in the first period, technological innovation created entirely new industries.

In the second time period, the newly created industries grew rapidly, compared to older industries because the older industries had lower demand elasticities, and as prices dropped, there was little increase in demand for older industry products.

In the third time period, regional economic growth depends on the continued development of new products, and the changing mix of industrial sectors brought about by technical change.

To the extent that a regional economy exhibits a high degree of technical change in indigenous small firms, the economy will exhibit a high degree of economic growth, described as increases in per capita incomes and personal per capita wealth.

To the extent that the regional economy is dependent upon global corporate technology macrostructure, the regional economy will exhibit a high degree of stagnant economic growth and job creation because the economic benefits of technological innovation are absorbed internally by the corporations located within the region.

Prior to 1992, the type of global trade policies promoted by the Republicans would not have been effective for the corporations because senior executives had inadequate methods for coordinating internal corporate management across national boundaries.

With the advent of the internet telecommunications technology, the Republican trade policies worked in tandem with the new internet communication technology (ICT), to allow corporations to both manage their global enterprises more effectively, and to internalize the revenues from global technology cluster chains.

This development in ICT explains part of the reason why corporate profits have been historically high, since the implementation of the trade policies, at the same time that the American economy has been so weak.

The economic spillover effects, called income and employment multipliers, before 1992, have been internalized inside the corporate value chains.

The internet technologies were both a cause of the corporations to seek global markets because competitors were using the technology, and also an enabling technology that destroyed American technological superiority.

When the Republicans abdicated freedom, and passed the new trade laws, the economy of America lost its ability to generate jobs and economic growth. That outcome would not have been effective prior to the adoption of ICT as a management tool by senior executives in the global corporations.

The introduction of ICT in the world economy, occurring at the very same moment in history as the Republican trade policies, disrupted the primary set of traditional conditions that global corporations were used to, in terms of making money.

In the very recent past, (prior to 1987), global corporations needed stable local political environments and stable global markets in order to rely on long-run production processes so that output per unit of input increased. They needed stable product-life cycles for mass-produced, finished goods in order to set prices at a target rate of profit. They needed stable, predictable markets to control the length of time a given production technology in a manufacturing unit would remain competitive.

The emergence of ICT, as the social shaping school theorists suggest, changed those traditional assumptions about global operations. When global corporations adopt ICT as an input factor of production, the ICT improves internal productivity, but also affects global market competitive conditions, because all global corporations are also simultaneously adopting the same technology.

Boland and Tenkasi note that "Lateral-flexible organizational form relies on peer-to-peer collaboration (as opposed to vertical hierarchy) in achieving organizational objectives...the relentless pace of change in market expectations means that all organizations will increasingly rely on creating new knowledge and adopting lateral organizational form."

They offer an explanation that organizations will adopt a lateral organizational form. The two concepts, organizational form, and relentless pace of change, appear to be connected, presumably through the key explanatory variable of "organizational objectives," which is left undefined by the writers.

Marshall Poole also fits his observations of ICT into the four dimensions of change as outlined by Fulk and DeSanctis. He writes that "organizations will use information technology to integrate across functions, re-engineer production and service processes, and create increased interdependence among activities."

The result will cause a "speed up in production and response time." According to Poole, the speed up in production and response time will cause organizations to adopt flexible, flat hierarchies that feature team-based work.

The major changes in the economy that result from the adoption of ICT in global corporations can be summarized as:
- Restructuring to the corporation's core technology and market efficency, with ensuing layoffs and downsizing.
- Outsourcing components of the manufacturing process,
- Relying upon small, flexible, highly automated manufacturing firms, primarily located in major metropolitan areas of the world.

The outsourcing is made possible by the implementation of ICT that Rosenberg called "telematics."

Fast product cycles and very limited response time to changes in market demand, especially for final, finished goods, that are increasingly sold in mass, global markets that are linked through the communication networks of the new information communication technology (ICT), primarily internet based marketplaces.

Internal corporate venture capital investments are aimed at either protecting the corporation's own core technological competency or extending that core competency along compatible new technology paths for new products.

Productivity improvements related to the adoption of ICT on a global scale generally means "loss of jobs and loss of incomes" for ordinary Americans.

In an effort to better understand the puzzle of why ICT has been accompanied by loss of jobs and incomes, the National Science Foundation commissioned a research project and retained Marc Uri Porat to conduct the investigation. His work, *The Information Economy: Definition and Measurement*, provides a useful intellectual framework for understanding what information communication technology is.

His method placed ICT within the framework of an econometric input-output model in order to explain how ICT in one sector affects other industrial sectors.

Porat began his investigation by defining information flows within an economy in terms of knowledge flows about markets. The end product that is useful, according to Porat, is the knowledge that is derived from information.

Knowledge, as a mental construct, can be further defined in terms of existing markets and existing production techniques in a current period of time, as contrasted with new knowledge in a market, which involves the mental property of insight, imagination, and the sorting of mental images.

This second type of "new" knowledge is more important as it relates to the imagination of entrepreneurs and the effect it has on the process of new venture creation in a future period of time.

Deriving knowledge from information flows within the economy is not an easy task. Interpreting the significance of information requires a prior intellectual construct to sort the information into units that can be discarded and units of information that can be gated through for further analysis.

As Porat points out, "One of the most difficult (and lucrative) problems in an information rich world is developing skills to package information that is useful: in the right form, at the right place and the right time."

Porat's analysis made an important distinction between ICT, as an input to a firm's production function and the "new" knowledge that potentially can be derived from ICT. In order to observe ICT in its role as an input to the firm's production function, Porat placed the "information as knowledge" flows into the logical structure of input-output analysis.

His logic in using the input-output model was that "Most information markets require a chain of output from other information industries in order to deliver the final product." This application of I-O is slightly different than the conventional use of I-O, which generally focuses on the impact that a change in final demand will have on intermediate demand.

In Porat's case, he used I-O to trace information flows from the start of the production process all the way to the end final demand for finished goods, rather than as the conventional case of starting with final demand and working backwards towards the start. This logical chronological sequence, that Porat calls the "chain of output," allows for a better understanding of what ICT is, from a static equilibrium perspective.

When information communication technology is viewed in an input-output relationship, it is easier to imagine how information, as an input, enters a production process, wherein something happens, and knowledge comes out as an output.

ICT, as seen as an input, has a simultaneous analog with other factors of production. In the case of ICT, the output is knowledge, while in the case of other factors, the output is a product. The input-output conceptual framework, deployed in conjunction with Porat's definition of "information as knowledge" allows Porat to ask two important questions.

First, he asks how interindustry information flows affect a firm's knowledge about existing markets. And, second, given a fixed production function, a fixed objective function, in a given period of time, how does current knowledge about markets affect a firm's decisions about the level of production, the type of production, and the type of finished product to produce in the next period of time.

The dilemma for global corporations, according to Porat, is that senior managers "...must await the decision of the marketplace (in the current period of time) before they can determine the level of output for the next period of time."

Porat's conceptual framework draws out this dilemma in terms of the continuously vexing management problem of "make in-house" or outsource. The input-output model allows ICT to be seen as an input, whose major contribution across all global industries is to compress the time frame of the next unit of time, as in the case with Lucent's optical router decision, to a matter of months, not years.

The result of this compression of time is the previously stated trend in outsourcing in global corporations. Porat describes and categorizes firms in relationship to their connection to the "information as knowledge" flows in the economy.

His three classes are:

- Markets for information, which consists of firms that produce knowledge or innovations.
- Information in markets, which consists of firms that are oriented to the search and coordination function within markets.
- Information processing and transmission infrastructure, which consists of firms which provide the technological networks upon which information flows.

Information flows in each class of firms will be different. Porat's classification allows the different effects of ICT, as described as an input to production, to be distinguished between the technical networks of computers, routers, gateways, etc.,

This is an important distinction between what ICT is, as a technology, and what it does, in terms of knowledge, that is explained by Porat's analysis. Technology is knowledge, and ICT is the technical network that connects information to knowledge. The use of ICT by global corporations allows them to rapidly gain a type of knowledge about the future direction of markets that they did not have in a previous time period.

They can then deploy that knowledge in a regional economic production strategy, which tends to disrupt the existing knowledge flows among local small firms within the metro regions.

However, as Porat's analytical framework points out, being connected is not the same thing as automatically deriving knowledge from the connection. Deriving knowledge, in the case of the global corporation, is essential for handling the uncertainty created by the unstable global markets. Corporations have a defined utility function for the use of information.

Porat's use of an input-output model that described information flows between industrial sectors was also useful for understanding the "productivity" puzzle in the late 1970s. By breaking the economy into his three-level classification scheme, based upon a firm's connection to the information markets, he opened the way to think about ICT in a new way. The new production efficiency associated with the information economy lay in Porat's insight about manager's awaiting the "verdict of the market."

The verdict of the market for what product to produce in the next unit of time and the selection of the correct production process to produce the product arises in new ventures, not in the existing firms being studied under conditions of general equilibrium.

In trying to solve the productivity problem. the economics profession was looking for productivity gains associated with ICT in the wrong place, primarily because that is where their theory told them to look.

It is the combination of these trends in ICT, as viewed as a technological input, that creates the market instability and uncertainty in the minds of the senior managers over how to react. The value of Porat's intellectual framework is that it allows for an easy-to-understand way to see how information as knowledge can easily flow between global corporations in the same industrial sectors.

The uncertainty and instability in global markets is created because, as the information as knowledge flows across industrial sectors, everyone sees the same information as everyone else, at the very same moment in time. Everyone is connected. Everyone has access to a global macro structure of communication and production technology.

Porat identified ICT as a factor of production that affected the way that information technology (IT) corporations conducted operations. His classification scheme for IT firms, as it related to selling their services in the information market, allowed for a better understanding of how easily information flowed across industrial sectors, and how it had different effects on different sectors.

He did not address how ICT affected global corporations specifically, nor how the implementation of ICT in competitor enterprises tends to disrupt the conditions of market stability that global corporations need in order to be profitable.

As noted by Bertuglia and his colleagues in *Innovative Behavior In Space and Time*, ICT makes competing on the basis of price nearly impossible. "Cost leadership erodes in global markets, because the common production technology drives profits to zero and that causes product life cycles to be short."

Feldman and Kulay, in *Innovation and Strategy in Space: Towards a Location Theory of the Firm*, extend the analysis of Bertuglia. They note that the multinational corporation is engaged in a global strategy of assessing the requirements of each component of production, finding the most appropriate location and then linking the activities together, (through ICT), to produce the product.

The result of ICT, they note, "has been a dramatic shortening of the product life cycles. New technological breakthroughs can make established products obsolete virtually overnight... product innovation is a multi-phase process which integrates various types of expertise within the organization and incorporates feedback between proucers and their suppliers and product users."

Part of the uncertainty and instability is related to ICT as a technical factor of production, and part of it arises from what ICT does in terms of the mental transformation of information into knowledge.

The part of ICT technology that is contributing to global market profit uncertainty and product cycle instability is the part that creates the non-symmetrical relationship between global corporations and elected representatives in metro regions.

Corporations need to impose some order and certainty in the direction of technology in order to reap the mass-market benefits of the global marketplace. In order to impose global order, they need metro regions to perform certain uniform types of market functions.

The urge for regional political control by multinational corporations is occurring at the same time that the trends in technology allow for the political control to be achieved. The first trend is towards telecommunication network convergence. The convergence in technology of networks is a result of the acceptance of common protocols and commonly adopted international standards of transmitting information.

As described by Steven Shepard, the commonly adopted Internet Protocol (IP) of addressing the destination of information packets, overlaid onto the logical virtual networks of asynchronous transfer mode (ATM), means that all firms that make infrastructure equipment are moving, simultaneously, to a network that is highly interoperable, no matter what equipment the vendor sells to the end user.

In this case, the purchasing manager in a global corporation making a decision between vendors in any part of the world can assume that prices offered by the vendors will be the same.

The end result of the ICT infrastructure technology is that the cost of doing business is the same in every part of the globe. The significance and implication for American economic welfare is that location of a branch plant in America in the production process does not matter.

Second, from a technical factor, the speed of transmission in a network is increasing at the same time that the quality of service in transmission is improving. Walter Goralski describes how the recent innovation in multiple protocol label switching (MPLS) allows any local area network to be connected to any other network in the world with extraordinarily fast high quality of service information flows.

This means that, in terms of technology, each node on the network throughout the world sees the same information at about the same period of time. In terms of anticipating what a competitor may do with the information, there is no time to react to the existing threat based upon prices.

Finally, in an international network of computers that features interoperability and open standards, once any single computer is assigned a unique IP address, linking that computer to the global network of computers is a simple matter of a connection. Everyone, everywhere, in the global economic macrostructure, is going to be connected, technologically.

The urge to create stability in global markets tends to undermine the price adjustment mechanism of competition, an essential element of how free markets create production efficiency. Diagram 5.1 is a schematic representation of the logical linkage between global market instability created by ICT.

Diagram 6.1. Global Market Instability Caused by ICT

Change in Global Market->	Predicted Corporate Behavior
ICT Internet becomes Walrasian Auctioneer of Global e-commerce market	More B-to-B, more B-to-C based single exchange oriented transactions. Does not require on-going trust relationship with client Market share in long term not important as global strategy
Global mass market of consumption not tied to global mass production -first to market with new product -increased focus on R & D that finds new product first	Seek to stabilize revenues within core technical competency through: -Control over protocols/standards that favor core technology -Licensing and certification standards -Political manipulation -Trade associations aimed at core technical competency in strategic partners
Increased risk associated with any investment aimed at future periods of time	Seek to protect core technical competency through: -Mergers/acquistions along technical path -Focused R & D -Venture Capital investments in core and complementary technologies -Cartel-like alliances with common core technology partners Seek new sources of profits from: -Capital gains from sale of subsidiaries and internally created new ventures. -Capital gains from investments in ventures in non-related industries

J. R. Hicks noted that under conditions of price competition, equilibrium could be reached, theoretically, if firms face rising marginal costs in production. In the face of declining marginal costs, firms may be able to achieve economies of scale in operation, leading eventually to monopoly.

He went on to note that "...the only reason why marginal costs should increase is the increasing difficulty in controlling the enterprise, as the scale of production grows." The main benefit of ICT for corporations is that it allows decreasing difficulty in controlling the global operations, both across national borders and across global markets, thus leading to conditions of declining marginal costs.

One of the main effects of the application of ICT on the operations of a corporation is to reduce the costs of administering the corporation, no matter how large or how geographically dispersed it may be.

The effect of ICT is to reduce costs for the individual corporation, while at the same time, if every global corporation is implementing ICT to remain competitive, the related effect is to make global cooperation among firms in the supply chain easier to accomplish. The ease of global cooperation in terms of extended supply chain outsourcing is enhanced if each metro region functions in a common regulatory and legal global environment.

A global firm that introduces ICT faces declining marginal costs in the command and control functions of administration. The earlier economic predictions of Hicks, and his contemporary, Joseph Schumpeter, were accurate that declining marginal costs would lead to increasing scale of operation. Corporations would be able to administer prices and to establish market monopoly by keeping competitors from entering the market.

Outsourcing, accompanied by the declining marginal costs caused by ICT, creates the heightened need to protect the firm's core technical competency from being disclosed inadvertently in the extended supply chain.

At the same time that global firms are using ICT to streamline corporate command and control operations in making goods, ICT is making global mass markets more alike in every country. The effect in the mass global markets means that the product life cycle for any single product has increased dramatically.

These two effects, the one in production and the one in the market, are taking place at a moment in history where political barriers to international trade are being removed, opening global markets to new trends in e-commerce such as business-to-business web sites.

These three factors combined mean that the prior terms of competition that required stable markets, long run production processes to get maximum output out of a production technique, and product differentiation as a strategy are now passé. It does not necessarily take a global corporate monopoly to extract monopoly-like profits anymore, as it would have in the period of time that Hicks was writing.

The new production technology of ICT in global market competition does not require mass production to serve global market demand. In the new global macrostructure, any small flexible unit of production, located anywhere in the world can be coordinated with any other of the corporation's units, and the price to manufacture the product, is the same.

The major factor of competition is not price, but control over technology in product evolution.

Diagram 6.2, entitled "What ICT Does To Corporate Operations and What That Means to a Corporation," is a schematic representation for how ICT affects the operations of a single hypothetical global corporation.

In order for senior managers in a corporation to transform information flow from ICT into knowledge, a prior mental construct in the brains of the senior corporate executives must frame the information.

Diagram 6.2. What ICT Does To Corporate Operations and What That Means to a Corporation

What ICT Does To Corporate Operations ->	What This Means To the Corporation
Declining marginal costs of production in command, control, and coordination	Marginal profit per unit of exchange goes up, if first to market.
Deconstruction of external value chain in intermediate suppliers and distributors	Loss of business/social communication network on products/processes
Creation of global macro structure in technology of production/communication	No comparative advantage in lowest cost producer in long run because all competitors have same costs of production
Deconstruction of internal communication networks by automation/integration of order flow/work flow/production and finances	Elimination of mid management internal career paths. No upward occupational mobility from technical/production to senior management No internal learning/institutional memory/new knowledge No employee allegiance/trust/loyalty to corporation No agents who bear "trust" to external organizations
Increased speed and increased access of common information/data sets to every division of corporation for coordination of work, setting global market strategy, allocation of financial resources, and internal accounting	Very small, relative to today, senior staff can control entire corporation. Tight management control over core technical competency

In his 1998 article, *Information Systems Use In Continuously Innovative Organizations*, Jonathan Allen called this the "problem framing" issue. The technology surrounding the firm's existing core competency tends to be the mental framing construct upon which knowledge is extracted from information. The extraction of knowledge requires the senior executives to ask the right questions for knowledge creation, which is a mental activity.

The reliance on existing core competency as the mental framing construct in global corporations will likely increase in the future, due to the value of "new knowledge" as it relates to the fast product life cycles. New knowledge is derived from mental insights and imagination, generally gained in social/business networks.

Jacky Swan noted, "Researchers on innovation argue that the innovation process is socially and societal embedded. An important aspect of the context for firms in an industry is the firm's links, both formal and informal, with a variety of other types of organizations." One of the most important informal social information links is with elected leaders in each metro region.

As a result of the restructuring and layoffs of middle management in global corporations, the global corporation will eventually be left with a very small group of senior managers, located at the international corporate headquarters. The middle managers previously performed much of the information gathering function in the social business network that created "new" knowledge in the corporation.

Those middle managers, especially in America, have been laid off, and replaced by the ICT networks that allow the senior executive to see and interpret new information.

The restructuring in corporations has eliminated the middle managers from this information gathering capability and has cut the senior managers off from the flow of information in the social/business networks that created new knowledge in the earlier period of time.

The senior managers still exercise command and control over the corporation's technical competency, using the channels of communication created by ICT. But, the information that they need as an input to their mental framing process has been disrupted.

In the absence of the previous flow of information from middle managers, the senior managers will increasingly rely upon their social and personal contacts with indigenous firms and local elected leaders to provide important information.

This is one reason why annual events, such as the one in Davos, are so important to senior global corporate executives as a meeting place to conduct business in private.

The senior managers need this type of event to make the face-to-face personal contacts with the elected leaders in order to coordinate corporate policy across national borders. The senior managers will use new knowledge to make strategic corporate investment decisions regarding the direction of corporate research and development.

The senior managers in all corporations will see information at the same time that every other smart global manager sees it. The key competitive advantage for any single corporation will be how fast they can turn the information into knowledge, and then, how fast they can turn that knowledge into a commercial product.

Global ICT networks create the conditions for a common technology of communication and production processes across organizational structures while at the same time, making global markets for finished goods more unstable as a result of the fast product life cycles.

The speed of information flow in ICT is accompanied by a reduced payback period for any new product created by corporate R & D and reduces the length of time a new product remains profitable. The new dynamic of the global market requires any single corporation to be first to market with a new product, and then first to market again, in the immediate future period of time.

However, as a result of restructuring to the core technical competency, the new goods are produced in a manufacturing process by many other corporations in the extended supply chain. The outsourcing tends to cut the corporation off from information about what the end users in the final demand marketplace think about the new products. Often, the senior managers know more about where their supply inputs are coming from than where their output is being sold.

The implementation of ICT created the potential conditions for an organizational "boundaryless" corporation through computer-based coordination of outsourcing parts of the production process.

The implementation of ICT allowed a global corporation to geographically decentralize the structure of operations and production while facilitating centralized command and control.

However, the same ICT that facilitates tighter command and control for any single corporation also creates the technology for dissipating the core technical competency of the global corporation.

The dissipation of proprietary intellectual property occurs in the extended supply chains because no single senior manage is certain exactly who his business partners are either in production or in marketing. If the unknown business partners are successful in stealing the core technological competency, then they may be able to appropriate the stream of revenue associated with the technology.

The corporation's core technology becomes the most important asset for deriving revenues, and it is generally protected by global agreements that protect intellectual property rights. Global standards for protecting the corporation's core intellectual property become much more important to the corporation than protecting national sovereignty. The importance of protecting the corporation becomes the maximand of the Republicans who represent the special interests of the corporation.

At the same time, ICT enhanced the need for more carefully defined corporate property rights on intellectual property in order that the correct, legitimate, party in the outsourced chain of exchange obtain only the limited legal revenues due from the exchange.

Because ICT in production facilitates a common global production technology and because common production technology causes the marginal price of a new product exchange to quickly approach zero profit, the value of the extended reach in the global supply chain is eroded by the prospect of zero profits from exchange transactions.

The fast product life cycles in global mass final demand markets create a priority for location of manufacturing and research and development in certain regional metropolitan markets. Some regional metro economies have business and social networks that produce information that is very valuable to the corporation's core technological competency.

Clayton Christensen and Michael Raynor have written extensively about the type of technological innovation that occurs in large multinational corporations. They note, in *The Innovator's Solution: Creating and Sustaining Successful Growth*, the imperative of technological innovation that occurs in a specific moment of time in a company's history. If the company happens to miss the historical opportunity, or to put it another way, if the senior managers fail to seize the technological moment, the future of the company is in serious jeopardy.

"If you fail once to deliver it," they warn, "the odds that you will ever be able to deliver it in the future are very low." The "it" they are referring to is technological innovation that causes growth in company revenues.

They cite their research on innovation that shows of the 172 companies under investigation, 95% experienced a period of stalled economic growth. After the period of stalled growth, "...only 4% were able to successfully reignite their growth even to a rate of 1% above GNP growth."

They point out that corporations can only prioritize innovations that promise improved profit margins relative to their current production costs. At the same time that the range of innovations is constrained to their existing cost structure, multinational corporations confront the fast dynamics of product obsolescence in the global market.

Marginal profits in the global market are rapidly headed to zero on any new product.

As Christensen and Raynor note, "When the relevant dimensions of your product performance is determined not by you but by the subsystems that you procure from your suppliers, it becomes difficult to earn anything more than subsistence returns in a product category that used to make a lot of money."

The type of economic growth sought by corporations from product innovation is not the same type of economic growth sought by regional leaders in a metro region.

The citizens of Kalamazoo need maximum rates of technological diversity, and product variety, born of hundreds of new small ventures in order to obtain very high rates of regional economic growth. That economic growth would not necessarily benefit the existing cost structure of production of General Motors, which would like to hang on to legacy profits from the status quo for as long as possible.

Their interests in technological innovation for senior managers of global corporations are non-symmetrical, and mutually incompatible, in the new world of ICT, with the goals of local elected representatives. It is part of a Big Republican Lie to suggest that what is good for General Motors is good for self-sustaining economic growth in Kalamazoo.

The global corporations have interests in technical change that is not consistent with either the regional elected leaders or even with the business social networks within the region that favor of the status quo. The global headquarters for the multinationals are located outside of the region, and the senior executives have no financial motivation to facilitate self-sustaining economic growth in any region they may happen to have a production unit.

This conflict between the needs of global corporations and the constitutional public purpose of individual freedom cannot be solved under the existing constitutional arrangement. The issue will not go away even if a new constitution that identifies freedom as the goal of the constitution is enacted.

To summarize, global corporations need the assets of regional metropolitan markets for several reasons. First, the social business networks of the metro region serve as a replacement for the social/business networks that the corporation used to have, internally, for creating new knowledge.

Second, the metro region's core technological cluster of industries acts as a reliable source of tax-payer subsidies that extend the corporation's core competency through collaborative R & D in regional universities and publicly funded non-profit research organizations.

These are not the same set of reasons why a regional metro community would need the location of global corporations for creating the conditions of regional wealth and economic growth.

Diagram 6.3, entitled "Prediction of How Unstable Global Market Will Affect Corporate Behavior," is a schematic description and prediction of how global corporations respond to the new risks associated with fast product life-cycles.

The implementation of ICT has created a new dynamic in the relationship between multinational corporations and metro economic regions. This new dynamic features a non-symmetrical relationship between the goals and needs of the global corporation for controlling technological innovation to serve the corporation's financial interests, and the metro regional community's need for diversity and variation in generating technological innovation.

Diagram 6.3. Prediction of How Unstable Global Market Will Affect Corporate Behavior

Market Instability ->	Increased Investment Risks ->	Increased Decision Uncertainty
Rate of product innovation increases.	What to produce in next period of time?	How to produce product?
Rapid technical change in production processes.	What core intellectual property to protect in R & D?	How to appropriate profits from short term exchanges on products derived from outsourced production? (property rights)
ICT standards/protocols change/unsettled.	What macro technological structure to adopt?	What strategic alliances/cartel/research collaboration to form?
Exchanges based on e-commerce short term (mass market demand shift).	No loyalty/trust/allegiance with clients on exchanges based on price.	How to continually derive profits from e-commerce exchange?
Exchanges base on e-commerce drive profits to zero after initial period (first to market).	Production processes and plant and equipment expenditures obsolete.	How to avoid dependency on profits derived from e-commerce exchange?
Global product liability not uniform across political boundaries.	Civil litigation/government regulation for actions of subsidiaries.	How to transfer risks to others in the global market?

From the perspective of the corporation, the common production process is related to knowing how technology in any one sector of production may be influencing technical change in another sector, which may ultimately affect the corporation's core technical competency.

Michael Best, in *The New Competition: Institutions of Industrial Restructuring*, describes this "new" knowledge spillover effect in terms of the difference between existing knowledge and new knowledge. In his view, new knowledge in a corporation is often gained through experience with machines and work processes, which he calls "thinking and doing" knowledge.

Best is correct in his emphasis of knowledge as the key future asset that will cause the greatest competition and conflict between corporations and regions. The effect of ICT on knowledge creation in a global market is an enduring fact of life. To the extent that there is a conflict between knowledge that benefits individual freedoms or serves to benefit corporations, then that conflict must be solved in the favor of free citizens.

Diagram 6.4 offers a summary of the six major conflicts between free citizens and the global corporation's need to control the flows of knowledge for their exclusive benefit.

Diagram 6.4. Summary of the Enduring Conflicts Over Knowledge Between Free Citizens and Corporations Caused by ICT

Global ICT networks create the conditions for a common technology of communication and production processes while at the same time, making global markets for finished goods more unstable. The new Areach" of ICT in accessing global markets is accompanied by a reduced payback period for any new product created by corporate R & D, and reduces the length of time existing new products remain profitable. The new dynamic of the global market requires any single corporation to be first to market, and then first to market again, in the immediate future period of time.

As a result of restructuring to the core technical competency in order to produce new goods, the global corporation undergoes outsourcing of parts of the manufacturing process and layoffs of middle managers. Middle managers are the most important resources of institutional knowledge of existing markets and technology. By restructuring, and layoffs, the corporation cuts itself off from the source of internal learning and new knowledge, while creating conditions of no loyalty to the corporation in the remaining staff, who are focused on protecting their own welfare, not the corporation's welfare.

ICTs create the potential conditions for "boundaryless" corporations through computer-based coordination of outsourcing parts of the production process, at the same time that it enhances the need for more carefully defined corporate property rights on intellectual property in order that the correct, legitimate, party in the outsourced chain of exchange appropriates legal profits from the exchange.

ICTs extend the "reach" of global corporations based upon market exchange, yet because ICTs facilitate common production technology, and because common production technology causes the price of the exchange to approach zero profit, the value of the extended reach is eroded by the prospect of zero profits from exchange transactions.

ICTs allow a global corporation to geographically decentralize the structure of operations and production while facilitating centralized command and control. The same ICT that facilitates tighter command and control for any single corporation also creates the technology for dissipating the core technical competency of the global corporation.

At the same time that ICTs make global mass markets unstable sources of profits, based upon exchange transactions of goods for final demand, it creates the conditions for making certain regional metropolitan markets more stable in terms of intermediate, inter industry trading relationships. Global corporations need the stability of regional metropolitan markets for several reasons, two of which are: as a replacement for the social/business networks that it used to have, internally, for creating new knowledge, and as a reliable source of creating technological progress in the corporation's core competency through collaborative R & D in a region=s core technological cluster of industries. These are not the same reasons why a regional market needs the location of global corporations for creating the conditions of regional wealth and economic growth.

Chapter 7. The Politics of Managing the Relationship Between An American Natural Rights Republic And American Global Corporations

Sean Willenz, in *The Rise of American Democracy,* opens up his study by addressing the absence of the "*res publica*" or the public thing to be pursued by Madison's conception of the constitution.

The absence of the *res publica* raises for Willenz, the overriding question of democracy in America: "Should unelected private interests, well-connected to government, be permitted to control, for their own benefit, the economic destiny of the entire nation?"

According to Willenz, under the set of constitutional rules promoted by Hamilton, "the idea that the private banking and business community should have special powers in deciding economic policy" was adopted. Without those special powers, according to Hamilton, the wealthy citizens would not have allegiance to the new nation, and without their allegiance, his concept of the free market system would not function well.

In the passage of the trade laws, to take an example, there was no res publica. Citizens were never told of the consequences that the Republican strategy would have on the unstated res publica of individual freedom.

The interests of citizens in the common wealth, were deliberately buried by the Republican political strategy to enact the trade legislation, and the citizens were kept structurally ignorant.

And, after the passage of the laws, when the domestic economy began to suffer and hemorrhage jobs, citizens expected Republicans to do something about it.

James Buchanan and Geoffrey Brennan, in *The Reason of Rules: Constitutional Political Economy*, have offered an interesting critique of the current constitution of America that suggests why the Republicans failed to defend freedom. They explain that national and local elected officials may have selfish personal interests that they promote, after they have been elected, as opposed to some conception of promoting the public good or the common wealth.

During the election period, the politicians make promises to coalitions of voters to obtain a majority of votes. After the election, they shift from their promises of serving various special interest coalitions, to using government resources to serve their own interests.

This is one explanation of why the special interest political system in America did not work to protect the common good of individual freedom. It explains why the Republican abdication was successful for corporations, after the trade laws were passed in 1992. Following Buchanan and Brennan, the current constitution has no rules for prohibiting this behavior, and more importantly, no procedures for the citizens to reclaim their lost freedom.

Essentially, Republicans at the national and local level represented their selfish personal interests by promoting the interests of their corporate special interests. They used their office in Washington to derive maximum financial benefits for themselves by attaching their own private utility function to the financial utility function of the global corporate special interests.

Buchanan and Brennan's argument also explains, for example, why the economic and financial welfare of black people has never improved since 1963, even though the Democrats always promise black people that they will fix the unfair capitalist system, if the Democrats win the next election.

After the black voters vote for the Democrats, the elected Democrats serve their own financial interests, becoming fabulously wealthy, and in the next election cycle repeat their promises to black voters.

As noted by Brennan and Buchanan, "Individuals are recognized to possess their own privately determined objectives, their own life plans, and these need not be common to all persons. In this setting, rules have the function of facilitating interactions among persons who may desire quite different things."

The main point of the Buchanan and Brennan model is that the conflict between global corporations and the sovereign rights of citizens must be resolved by constitutional rules. The set of problems that executives of large companies face in managing their global operations are not going away.

The current constitution does not address this conflict and citizens have no way of regaining their freedoms. The conflict must be managed in a way that serves the freedom of citizens in America, while providing mechanisms for domestic corporations to compete with foreign corporations.

Kenneth Arrow explains the outcome when the constitutional rules do not contain the res publica. In *Social Choice and Individual Values,* he begins with an analysis of how a society can avoid the logical problem of infinite regress. Arrow points out how individual preferences are aggregated into social decisions. In other words, the constitution must contain the first principles of whose welfare counts, and then explain exactly how to count that welfare, in order to determine the total social welfare.

As a point of contrast, Arrow emphasis is on how individual preferences are aggregated to come up with a total social welfare calculation. Socialists do not believe in aggregating individual preferences in favor of collective group preferences of their favored voting coalitions, such as blacks, gays, etc.

Arrow asked: "What values should be used to determine the shape of the social welfare function?" A social welfare function is a mathematical formula that describes the end goals of society, and helps to measure progress towards those goals. The welfare function mathematically specifies and defines the term "public purpose."

Arrow went on to answer his own question by showing, from a mathematical point of view, that for every known method of making collective political decisions, there was no possibility of arriving at a social welfare function that would be consistently valued, from one time period to the next, by the citizens who vote in the society.

In the absence of res publica, consistency in the ranking of end goals of a democratic society, Arrow concluded, was impossible. Consistency, according to Arrow, could be achieved in a dictatorship. What Arrow meant by the condition of dictatorship is the ability of one individual preference function to become the social preference ordering, regardless of the preference functions of the other individuals.

The only way out of the Arrow's paradox of tyranny is to assume in the preamble of the new constitution, that only individual's have a welfare function, and to require that the constitution contain an explicit statement of the ultimate goal to be achieved via the constitutional rules. If the constitution fails on either condition then Arrow's condition of non-dictatorship is violated.

If the end goals of society cannot be made subject to individual preference rankings, as Kenneth Arrow suggests, than upon the same logic, social welfare outcomes cannot be subject to individual preference rankings. The importance of Arrow's insight for a moral constitutional democracy is that only rules and laws, which flow from the priority of values established in the constitution, can be ranked according to individual preferences.

In other words, part of the future management issue involves managing the conflict of financial interest between the multinational corporation's needs for global standardization, which extends the global macrostructure across national boundaries, and individual freedom for citizens in a defined sovereign geographical territory.

This conflict goes to the heart of the problem global corporations are having in defining the boundaries of their corporate property rights to appropriate profits from intellectual property, after 2002, when they outsourced most of their production processes from American locations.

Corporate control over information flows allows for better control over proprietary intellectual property, which allows the corporate a better chance of obtaining monopoly profits. Open technology information flows, on the other hand, is a prerequisite condition of regional and national economic growth.

Using the political model suggested by Buchanan and Brennan, it would have been easy, prior to 1992, to analyze what the political objective function being maximized was by the trade policies.

But, in order to use their model to analyze the effects of the trade policies, it would have first been important to state what the res publica of the constitution was. Part of the task of this chapter is to explain the public purpose served by free people and free competitive markets in obtaining maximum social welfare.

This would be a useful exercise in drafting a new natural rights constitution because a new constitutional arrangement must confront the ongoing and enduring permanent feature of a global market.

Part of the task of this chapter is to explain how a constitutional arrangement based upon the goal of individual freedom would manage the government's relationship with the senior managers of global corporations.

The new constitutional rules need to be drafted based upon an understanding of what the global corporations need in order to function in a way that does not damage individual sovereignty or national sovereignty. The economic issue to be solved involves a goal of freedom and independency, as opposed to the current constitutional arrangement, which fosters political and economic dependency of citizens upon the decisions of the global corporations.

Digram 7.1 summarizes the four conflicts that must be managed in the future, if the new constitution contains the sole goal of securing and defending individual freedom.

Diagram 7.1. Summary of the Conflicts to Be Managed Between Free Citizens and Corporations

Type of Conflict	Regional Interest	Global Corporate Interest
Flows of technical information within region	Open flows to create wide range of new ventures	Private, proprietary flows to absorb internal benefits of technology
Flows of entrepreneurs from corporations to new ventures	Open flows, maximum new venture creation	Limited flows in order to protect core competency
Pathway of technical change in region	Maximum technical change and greatest diversity in new venture creation	Technical change directed to global corporation's core competency
Cultural/political values	Individual freedom, reward based upon individual merit, maximum individual risk-taking	Globalist/collectivist values oriented to using government to promote resolution of market based conflicts

A useful starting place to investigate the management of the conflicts is with Stephen Kobrin, in *Multinational Corporation: The Protest Movement and the Future of Global Governance*, where he described corporate globalism in terms of increasing dependency of the regional economy on the technological innovation associated with multinational corporations.

"Globalization is a transition from a world ordered geographically...to an a-territorial, networked mode of organization." Korbin states that the "...dependent developing countries have little, if any, control over critical decisions affecting their economies and their societies."

Geoffrey Jones also touches on the relationship between technological dependency and the loss of territorial sovereignty in *Multinational and Global Capitalism: From The Nineteenth to the Twenty-First Century*. He states, "The borders of multinational corporations and nation states are not, by definition, identical. As a result, governments are confronted by economic entities whose ultimate control and ownership lies beyond their borders, while firms face multiple jurisdictions rooted in different political systems."

Jones calls this condition "jurisdictional asymmetry," as seen from the eyes of the senior executives in multinational corporations. The jurisdictional asymmetry can be overcome, from the global corporate perspective, when there are not so many sovereign nations to deal with, and the ones that do matter willingly subjugate their national sovereignty to the global corporate management system.

As a result of the political influence of multinational executives, the host regional economies generally lose political control and democratic accountability over the future direction of the regional economy. Usha Haley, in *Multinational Corporations In Political Environments: Ethics, Values and Strategies,* has called the loss of economic and political sovereignty the "sovereignty at bay" effect.

In an interdependent global production process, the multinational corporations require uniform standards of trade and commerce in the political host regimes. "Therefore," writes Haley, "dependent development encourages authoritarian regimes in host states and creates alliances between multinational (executives) and domestic reactionary elites."

The main problem, prior to 1992, from the perspective of the multinational corporations, was that there were just too many sovereign national governments involved in the global market that inhibited the global technological uniformity that they needed.

The way the new trade laws were passed, in conjunction with the new forms of ICT, created the conditions of authoritarian regimes, both in the United States, with the appearance of elected representatives who choose not to follow rules, and in foreign countries, where there are no rules.

William Greider, in his article, *A New Giant Sucking Sound,* describes the new global market "the race to the bottom." "Globalization is entering a fateful new stage," writes Greider, "in which the competitive perils intensify for the low-wage developing countries much like the continuing pressures on high-wage manufacturing workers in the United States...As one economy after another sinks into contraction, output subsides nearly everywhere..."

Martin Wolf, in *Why Globalization Works*, states, "Not only is it very difficult (for most citizens) to know what is going on, but most citizens have no interest in doing so. They are "rationally ignorant..." He states, "It is impossible for the citizenry to reach sensible decisions on most of the matters that come before governments."

The problem, as seen by Wolf, is not only that multinational corporations exert unelected, unaccountable and undemocratic control over economic growth in America. The main problem is that the functioning of the global economy in the hands of the corporate leaders, is invisible, and deliberately so, from the way the current special interest political system operates.

One part of the new constitutional arrangement is to promote the maximum rate of entrepreneurial activity, free from corporate domination and control. Prior to 2002, the supply of entrepreneurs for the new technology ventures in America were drawn from the ranks of middle managers in existing large corporations. The agents who absorbed new technological knowledge on behalf of the corporation, were the very same personnel who would leave to create a new venture.

Those agents were always leaving, and taking their knowledge with them, the corporation's objective of appropriate profits from technological knowledge will become more difficult. Part of the symbiosis between university research and global corporations was designed to overcome this issue, as seen by the financial needs of the corporations by channeling research commercialization directly into the corporation.

Part of the explanation for the dramatically reduced rates of new venture creation and low rates of venture capital investment in the domestic U. S. economy, after 2002, is related to the effectiveness of Republican policies and rules that tended to restrict occupational mobility of the latent supply of entrepreneurs.

The public's interest in economic growth, on the other hand, is served when middle managers and latent entrepreneurs have the greatest occupational mobility and freedom to create new ventures.

In their review of research on entrepreneurship, Bruno and Tyebjee list the main factors that seem to influence the supply of entrepreneurs in a metro region. As cited in *The Encyclopedia of Entrepreneurship*, the top three factors are:
- The supply of venture capital in the region..
- The presence of experienced entrepreneurs.
- A supply of technically skilled workers.

The conclusion drawn from their review is that the source of new entrepreneurs is the supply that potentially exists in the personnel ranks of existing firms. In many of the metro regions they reviewed, those existing firms are branch operations of multinational corporations who located the branch in that region to absorb the benefits of the region's technological knowledge.

Pier Saviotti, in *Technological Evolution, Variety, and The Economy*, describes why the supply of entrepreneurs is important to the process of technical change in a region. "The knowledge of engineers, scientists, managers, technicians, etc., involved in the implementation of the technology becomes specialized around the process, technical, and service characteristics used. This specialization creates networks of communication and power which reinforce the stability of the artifact dimension of the technology."

In other words, an existing social-business network of skilled individuals, working in a production unit, share some specialized knowledge about a process. Within this network, one would expect that potential entrepreneurs meet with each other and discuss the feasibility of starting a new venture, based upon their technical knowledge and their understanding of the potential market for the products produced.

Chinitz also identified the supply of entrepreneurs in a metro region as a causal factor in regional economic growth. Cited in Feser's work, *Enterprises, External Economies and Economic Development*, Chinitz, in 1961, drew a connection between the location of multinational corporations and the type of economic growth that could occur in a distinct metro region.

Chinitz hypothesized that the "...entrepreneurial supply curve is also a functionof certain traditions and elements of social structure which are heavily influenced by the character of the area's historic specializations."

He went on to elaborate that "...in competitively organized places, the potential for nurturing new, dynamic and innovative businesses is much greater than in those places where oligopolistic industries predominate."

The supply of entrepreneurs in a region provides an ingredient to the process of technical change that is absent in the framework of the existing old production units in a region.

In his historical review of technological innovation, Robert McAdams noted that economic historians share a widely held belief about the origins of venture capital in the eighteenth century.

In *Paths of Fire*, McAdams wrote "...all of the sources are in agreement that considerable increases in disposable wealth came into the hands of a substantial elite during the later part of the eighteenth century. Perhaps it is not so much their diversified and growing desires as consumers that quickened the pace of technological advance (during that era) but rather the increasing supply of potential venture capital for which this elite was beginning more aggressively to seek new avenues for profitable investment."

According to McAdams in *Paths of Fire*, the entrepreneurs have a "creative vision" in their capacity to "anticipate a new convergence of consumer preferences and technological possibilities."

Peter Temin makes this same point in his article, *Entrepreneurs and Managers*. He states that:
"... entrepreneurs are the agents of change, ...(they) see new opportunities, invent new machines, discover new markets, ...(they) perform a different function from that of the manager, who works within a known technology, organization, and market."

The entrepreneur is the agent that links the unknown future of consumer preferences to technological possibilities, the result of which is economic growth. Managers of multinational corporate branch plants, on the other hand, see the day to day routine as the most important factor that determines their financial reward within the corporation. The standardization of the work process is something that is measurable, and that is how they are rewarded.

In making the distinction between unknown costs and risks of the future, and the known costs and risks in the existing old production unit, Temin and McAdams hit upon the single greatest economic contribution that entrepreneurs make to the evolution of regional technical change.

Entrepreneurs perform the economic function of creating the future markets by imagining how that market will work. They provide the guesses of prices and profits, and how technological change in production units will interact with, as yet unseen, consumer preferences. This ability of entrepreneurs is the American res publica, on a grand scale.

The entrepreneurs are a part of a regional social-business network, whose participants communicate with each other. Regional economists call these larger social networks, "regional industrial clusters."

Entrepreneurs may be able to leave the old production units in order to create new ventures, using the knowledge they gained about how things work, and with ideas about how to make the new venture more productive than the older units. The new ventures would probably be more productive and achieve higher overall production output per unit of input than the older units.

To the extent that the region has a high rate, or pace of technical learning, and has accumulated technical knowledge about production, it will have a high rate of technical change in production processes, and consequently, a high rate of economic growth. However, the combination of innovating firms, the presence of social-business networks, and the accumulation of technological knowledge are not distributed uniformly across regions.

In contrast, the branch plant managers in existing firms do not create a future market; they manage the enterprise based upon the prices and profits of the status quo market. While multinational firms need technological innovation, they need it as a resource input to strengthen their existing core technology and to enhance their current production process. They need technological innovation that they can control in the existing market so that it contributes to their revenues in the status quo future market.

As a result of locating in the region to absorb some of the benefits, the corporation begins a process of venture capital investments and research collaboration, oriented to the corporation's own core technical competency. This orientation to a private core competency is contrary to the diversification in industrial sectors that arises from technical change not influenced by global corporations.

From this perspective, regional economic development is described as a process that occurs as a result of diversification of both products and industrial sectors in a metropolitan area. The diversification is caused by technical change in production processes, which increases regional productivity. The improved productivity creates new flows of income and creates new pools of venture capital, which can potentially be invested in a second generation of new ventures.

The greater the rate of knowledge diffusion and absorption by small regional firms within the regional industrial cluster, the greater the rate of regional self-sustaining economic growth. The greater rates of economic growth are caused by the entrepreneurs, not by corporations, and not by government agents.

Sectors within a region may adopt a common technological paradigm in production techniques, independent of whether those sectors trade with each other. The degree of technological closeness, or the presence of a technological cluster, is related to both the process of knowledge diffusion and absorption, as well as to a third phenomenon, the development of collaborative relationships among sectors.

To the extent that a regional economy is characterized by technological closeness in production techniques, the rate of collaborative relationships will increase.

The greater the rate of collaboration among firms, the greater the number of new ventures created in service and supply industries, and the greater the level of outsourcing of discrete production processes in new manufacturing ventures.

Pasinetti's model, described in *Structural Change and Economic Growth: A Theoretical Essay On The Dynamics of The Wealth of Nation,* is useful for explaining the power of venture capital investments to determine the pathway of regional economic growth. In his work, Pasinetti describes a change in productivity brought about by technical change. The change in productivity "releases" a stream of new income, and also, creates a new demand for capital equipment and machinery.

Pasinetti's model predicts that the capital/output ratio of an economy will increase over time as a reflection of the increasing regional productivity. According to Pasinetti, technical change is always labor reducing and capital intensive in its effect on the production process.

He defines the capital/output ratio as the amount of new investment in the production process required to achieve a one-unit increase in output. In other words, he describes it in terms that can be applied to an input-output relationship.

Drawing upon the work of Passinetti, technical change is always capital intensive and labor saving in its effect. To the extent that trends in capital intensity can be reflected in the purchase and installation of machinery and equipment in new manufacturing ventures, there will be changes in the value-added flow of income in the row vector related to capital and entrepreneurial services.

The increased flows to the value-added row form the basis of a potential supply of venture capital in the region, which may, or may not, be reinvested by venture capitalists in subsequent generations of new ventures.

Capital for investment in the next generation of new ventures becomes, in other words, a regionally-produced means of production that becomes an intermediate input to reproduce a supply of investment capital in subsequent periods. The economic relationship is between investments in capital equipment in the first time period and an increase in value-added in the second time period.

Whoever, or whatever political force captures control over the deployment of this capital in the second time period as a source of investment in new ventures, will therefore establish a strangle-hold on the direction of technological change, and consequently, gain control over the direction of regional economic growth.

The change in value-added flowing to capital and entrepreneurial services, over the two periods of time under investigation potentially could create entirely new sectors in the region. The term value-added used in this context describes profits from capital gain exit events that occur in time period two.

To the extent that venture capital is invested in new ventures during the interval of time under investigation, the most recent transaction matrix will contain new rows and columns, and the technical coefficients from the earlier period will be larger in the second matrix for the sectors experiencing the highest rates of technical change.

Jane Jacobs identified a certain type of market configuration in metro regions that tended to promote a certain type of entrepreneurial economic growth. In *Cities and The Wealth of Nations: Principles of Economic Life,* she noted that it did not really matter whether the city market was based primarily on consumer retail purchases or on interindustry purchases between firms. The primary ingredient for regional economic growth that she identified were city markets that were diverse and concentrated.

In her research, she listed the factors she found in these diverse and concentrated city markets as:
- Huge collections of little firms,
- The symbiosis between the little firms in markets,
- The ease of breakaways of workers from older enterprises to new entrepreneurial ventures,
- The flexibility in the use of technology by little firms,
- The economies in production between the little firms, efficiencies in markets, and adaptive behavior in the face of novelty by the little firms

As new ventures are created, the interindustry buying and selling relationships among the small new ventures strengthen over time as production units communicate with each other over how things in the regional market work. As they communicate with each other, they are creating the new intermediate demand market place, generally called the regional supply chain.

These types of regional supply chain relationships create a cumulative feedback mechanism of technical change that contributes to the earlier feedback mechanism between the changing consumer preferences and the spending of incomes at the regional level between two time periods. These mechanisms are based upon social networks and not price movements that are adjusting the economy to equilibrium.

Young has noted that not all increased supply chain relationships in a city market contribute to regional self-sustaining economic growth. Cited in *Endogenous Growth Theory*, he makes the distinction between horizontal supply chain relationships, which "..add to the number of independent sectors over which research must be spread." He contrasts those relationships to vertical supply chain relationships "...which are primarily quality improving."

Saviotti, in *Technological Evolution, Variety, and The Economy*, extends this linkage between geographical place and technical change by introducing the concept of a "technological cluster" of firms in an area that share a common production technology. Saviotti's concept of clusters is close to what Marshall had in mind on his concept of industrial districts.

According to Saviotti, a region's path of economic development tends to converge towards common practices and product features. This trend toward a common set of technical knowledge contributes to an increase in productivity of existing firms, and as a result of the increased productivity, resources are "freed."

The resources which are freed from the existing system of regional production generate completely new production technologies. The idea that resources are "freed" from the existing production system is also found in Schumpeter and Leontief.

In the case of Saviotti, the freed resources function to push the regional production possibilities frontier outward, a conventional explanation of regional economic growth. In addition to pushing the frontier out, the new technologies also raise the overall industrial "variety" of the region, which is the same concept that Smith had in mind when he discussed the "extent" of the market. Variety, in this case, means increased intermediate demand transactions among the firms within the industrial cluster.

Saviotti notes that innovative firms "...tend to cluster in those (areas) that were already innovating countries.. .this specificity can not be explained by factor endowments, but is more likely to be caused by specific institutional configurations, and by the cumulative, local and specific character of the knowledge that the institutions possess."

A particular type of configuration of firms, led by multinational branch operations, may cause the benefits of technological innovation to be internally directed to the corporation and not to the broader society. In this case, the regional income and employment multiplier effect associated with extensive inter-firm trading relationships is circumscribed.

Bertuglia, in *Innovative Behavior In Space and Time*, noted that in an "urban context, the existence of forward and backward linkages between industrial and service sectors means that new innovations may have substantial multiplier effects on the whole urban economy." The hypothesized spread of benefits to the rest of the economy, however, does not occur under a configuration of firms where the multinational corporation has become the dominant actor in the regional industrial cluster.

The limited spread of economic benefits associated with the dominant multinational corporation technological innovation causes a peculiar type of regional economic growth to occur. The regional economy becomes dependent on multinational corporations for creating technological innovation. The economic dependency extends to a political dependency on the corporation for continuing to reside in the region, which gives the corporation power to extract concessions from the local citizens.

The profits associated with that form of technological innovation are absorbed by the corporation's owners and re-invested in a global strategy according to the needs of the corporation.

Neil Alderman, in *Local Product Development Trajectories: Engineering Establishments in Three Contrasting Regions*, calls the outcome associated with multinational corporate technological dominance, "path dependency."

His principal hypothesis was "...that different conditions in the regions with radically differing histories and industrial and organizational structures would give rise to different types of technological trajectory at the local level." Technical change in the region depended on the creation of technological knowledge, which is then transformed into commercially viable new products.

If the multinational corporations gain control over this knowledge creation process, they gain control over the region's path of technological innovation.

According to Morroni, the machines and capital equipment of an old production unit, in time period one, are technically indivisible, in the sense that, once in place on the factory floor, it is difficult for senior managers of the branch operations to adapt the equipment to changing demand conditions.

The investment in the equipment represents a fixed-cost, and that fixed-cost means that the equipment is not adaptable to changes in the volume, or output, of production if consumer preferences change.

In *Endogenous Growth Theory*, Aghion and Howitt use conventional economic theory to explain the relationship between profit reinvestment and innovation that occurs at the regional level when this particular configuration of firms occurs. They note that "...capital accumulation and innovation are complementary processes."

"More capital accumulation," they continue, "stimulates innovation by raising the equilibrium flow of profits, just as more innovation stimulates capital accumulation by raising the rate of productivity growth... without innovation, diminishing returns would choke off net income and without net investments, the rising cost would choke off innovation."

As Minsky pointed out in his article on managed global capitalism, regional economic development is a social process, which is influenced by what social actors, like venture capitalists, decide to do with their wealth. Sometimes, the local venture capitalists in a region have a business-social network that operates independently of the business-social network of the traditional power elite of multinational corporations.

Technical change at the regional level causes economic growth to occur as a result of the capital investment process in new ventures. In an earlier period of time, if venture capitalists in the region invest in new ventures, those new ventures may create a new regional intermediate demand supply chain in a later time period.

Economic growth occurs when incomes and production in the region increase as a direct result of the creation of the regional interindustry supply chains. The cause of the increase in supply chain relationships is the capital investment process in the earlier period in new ventures.

In any industrial district, or industrial cluster, the more firms that are tied into a common production technology via intermediate demand supply chain trading relationships, the faster a new production technology is diffused throughout the business and social networks of the regional economy.

This prediction about economic growth is consistent with the model of technical change developed by Rosenberg, who suggested that the existence of technologically close clusters of firms is related to the input-output concept of forward and backward linkages. Rosenberg's model states that there are flows of new equipment and materials within a cluster that generate a vastly disproportionate level of technical change and productivity growth in the economy.

Morroni's model, described in *Production Process and Technical Change*, tends to supplement and support Rosenberg's concept of forward and backward linkages by introducing the concept of complementary relationships.

In Morroni's model, there is a "constellation" of firms with a leading firm, and a cluster of complementary organizations, or a "network" of independent firms with collaborative relationships...The complementary relationships are determined by economic conditions, the respective chemical-physical and technical characteristics, the knowledge possessed by members of the production unit, prevailing rules and habitual practices and specific characteristics of the market."

Some of the complementary relationships described by Morroni would be captured in the input-output model as changes in the technical coefficients of service sector businesses, such as finance, law, real estate, and insurance.

Some of the collaborative relationships would be described as increases in intermediate purchase between sectors over two periods of time. Some of the relationships dealing with increased communication, changing habits, and knowledge flow would not be described in the input-output model.

Under conditions of fast technical change, it would be most rational for an entrepreneur to build the least cost, smallest, most flexible production unit possible, consistent with his expectations for how consumer preferences will change.

Morroni's model identified this preference for flexible automated production units as a result of the uncertainty the entrepreneur faced in making his choice of technique decision for his new production unit. He suggests that the one of the main characteristics of the recent trend to computer automated production techniques in manufacturing is an increase in the flow of information between people and between machines.

The increased information flow is related to the increased flexibility because of the "development of complementary strategic and cooperative relations with other firms in the regional industrial cluster. Through a telematic ICT network, a firm can acquire its semi-finished goods and production services, and thus enrich its production mix.

The increased production flexibility caused by ICT is not simply limited to "just-in-time" inventory control, but to a greater dependence of a single new unit on a greater range of intermediate input suppliers.

The greater the rate of technical absorption in the region resulting from the formation of new production units that have "best practice" production technology, the greater the level of interindustry dependency, as more of the total production process is out-sourced or in-sourced to other regional firms who share the common regional macrostructure. The characteristic of increased intermediate demand relationships is consistent with what Adam Smith called increasing the extent of the market. This increased flexibility is facilitated by the trends toward automated production techniques and computer information flows.

David Landes, In *The Wealth and Poverty of Nations,* wrote, "If we learn anything from the history of economic development, it is that culture makes all the difference. In the pursuit of wealth, failure or success are ultimately determined from within, not imposed from outside."

Landes identified the social/institutional variables that, historically, seemed to contribute to the wealth of nations. These variables were:
- private property rights,
- individual civil rights,
- legal rights of contract,
- consistently stable institutions of government with peaceful measures for the transfer of power,

These values can be protected by a constitution that states that individual freedom is the ultimate goal of government. In drafting a new constitution, the ultimate conflicts that need to be checked and balanced are not private financial interests in the system devised by Madison and Hamilton.

Their constitutional arrangement was designed to check and balance special interests, not check and balance socialism versus freedom. The insurmountable flaw in Madison's special interest constitutional arrangement is that there is no special interest that defends the public interest of individual freedom.

That new constitution will probably be best suited for a type of regional-nation state government, that allows the federal government to defend the national sovereign interests, while freeing up citizens at the regional metro level to pursue their regional economic interests.

The priority for the framers of the new constitution is to guarantee freedom of citizens, while protecting the ability of domestic multinational corporations to compete on the global markets, if, and only if, that competition benefits the citizens of the domestic economy.

Individual freedom is intertwined with the workings of the free market, and private property. When the Republicans failed to defend freedom, the benefits of the free market economy were lost for the great majority of Americans.

The next constitution must aim both at never letting this type of special interest sabotage to occur again, while providing citizens the democratic means to reclaim their liberty, if it does.

The principles of the American natural rights republic are contained in the events and documents related to the Second Continental Congress, of 1775. The Articles of Confederation were based upon the principles of natural rights expressed by Thomas Jefferson, in the Declaration.

Restoring the American natural rights republic means overthrowing the flawed document of 1787, and restoring the principles of natural rights contained in the Declaration of Independence. In the same manner that the Founding Federalists overthrew the Articles of Confederation, the new constitution restores the government that the colonists originally intended to create.

The Second Continental Congress convened on May 10, 1775, at Philadelphia's State House. Many of the same 56 delegates who attended the First Continental Congress of 1774, were in attendance at the second, including Benjamin Franklin of Pennsylvania and John Hancock of Massachusetts.

For its first year in operation, the Second Continental Congress managed the war effort against the British. On June 14, 1775, the Congress voted to create the Continental Army out of the militia units around Boston and appointed Congressman George Washington, of Virginia, as commanding general of the Continental Army.

On May 10, 1776, the Second Continental Congress adopted John Adams's resolution that each of the "united colonies adopt such government as shall, in the opinion of the representatives of the people, best conducive to the happiness and safety of their constituents in particular, and America in general."

Each colony then adopted its own state constitution, and all states, individually, declared their independence from the King.

On June 1st, The Second Continental Congress appointed a committee to draft a formal declaration of independence. Its members were John Adams of Massachusetts, Benjamin Franklin of Pennsylvania, Roger Sherman of Connecticut, Robert R. Livingston of New York and Thomas Jefferson of Virginia.

The document prepared by the committee was presented to Congress for review on June 28, 1776.

Richard Henry Lee's resolution for independence from Great Britain was presented to the Continental Congress on June 7. On July 2, 1776, the Second Continental Congress voted on Lee's resolution, and declared independence, on behalf of all the united states.

The vote on July 2, 1776 for Independence was unanimous, with only New York abstaining. In other words, both the states, acting individually, and the Continental Congress, acting collectively, declared independence from the King.

On August 20, 1776, the Second Continental Congress rejected the first draft of the Articles of Confederation, prepared by John Dickson, in June of 1776, and agreed to proceed with a second draft of the Articles. The first draft reflected the philosophy of the aristocratic class, based upon special class privileges in a consolidated central government.

The second draft of the Articles was drafted primarily by Thomas Burke, of North Carolina, and the draft was not a completed or finished document, when it was presented to the Second Continental Congress.

The second draft, of August 20, left four issues unresolved:
- the equal representation of all states in Congress.
- the basis of apportionment of common expenses.
- the grant of powers of the central government over western lands
- defining the location of sovereignty between the states and Congress.

Thomas Burke continued his work and proposed amendments to the second draft of the Articles that aimed at resolving the four issues.

Burke proposed:
- that all sovereign power was in the states separately.
- that the federal government held "expressly" enumerated powers…each state retains its sovereignty, freedom and independence.
- that any right which is not by this confederation "expressly" delegated to the United States in Congress assembled is retained by the states.
- Congress is to be made up of two bodies of delegates, the General Council, and Council of State, with one delegate from each state.
- All bills originate in the General Council, and are read 3 times and passed by a majority in the Council of State.
- Every law must be demonstrated to be within the powers "expressly delegated to Congress."

Part of Madison's duplicity in overthrowing the Articles with his Constitution of 1787, and then again, in the ensuing Bill of Rights, when he refused to insert the term expressly indicates his intent as early as 1785.

This term "expressly delegated" appears over and over again in the debates and resolutions of the Second Continental Congress, and Madison knew full well what the legal implications would be, if he allowed the full term, "expressly" to be inserted in the Constitution of 1787 or two years later, the Bill of Rights.

The Continental Congress adopted the Articles of Confederation, as amended by Burke, on November 15, 1777.

The first state to ratify the Articles of Confederation was Virginia on December 16, 1777; the thirteenth state to ratify was Maryland, on February 2, 1781.

The ratification of the Articles of Confederation by all 13 states of the new United States Congress occurred on March 1, 1781.

The principles of the American natural rights republic were clearly enunciated by Thomas Paine, in his series of pamphlets, the most well known of which is "Common Sense," first published on January 10, 1776. One of the most important principles of government, for Paine, was that the unalienable truths, identified by Jefferson in the Declaration, must be "knowable."

"Knowable" used in this historical context is related to knowable as a truth as derived from the Enlightenment rational school. Paine wrote that, "truth reached through the convictions of open inquiry and examination...universal moral truth, must be knowable."

Seven months later, when Jefferson wrote that "these truths are self-evident," the self evident truths were logical axioms, or most basic premises, from which deductive reasoning may proceed.

As Michael Zuckert explains, in The Natural Rights Republic, "...the evidentness of the truth is contained within the truths themselves...the truths are not affirmed to be in themselves self-evident, only to be held as such by the Americans...the truths are held as if self evident within the political community dedicated to making them effective. The truths serve as the bedrock or first principles of all political reasoning of the natural rights regime."

As an aside to explain an upcoming book, titled "A Civil Dissolution," the reason that Paine's basis of logic is so essential to the defeat of socialism, is that socialists reject the logic of the Enlightenment, and do not reason by logical truths. The socialists use a philosophy of logic called "moral relativism" which contains no independently objective criteria of truth.

For socialists, the truth of a proposition is in the degree and intensity of allegiance shown to the proposition by its adherents.

Socialism denies the absolute truth of natural rights. The moral relativism of global socialism, and its logical cousin, "Critical Legal Studies," can not exist in the same reality with self-evident truths. One, or the other, logical philosophy, must be vanquished from the field of battle.

For Paine, the new American government must be built on the truth, moral truth, not on power relationships that existed in the mixed British class system that Madison palmed off on America in 1787. For Paine, as for Jefferson, the truth was that God had granted citizens certain inalienable rights, commonly called "natural rights."

The new government, said Paine, "is derived solely from a sovereign people...mutually and reciprocally maintained principles of nature in society." As will be noted in chapter nine of this book, this single element of a natural rights republic, the "consent of the governed" is the glue that binds citizens together to obey the constitutional rules that they give to themselves.

The one duty that falls equally on all persons, wrote Paine, is the duty to defend and honor the principle of equal rights. Liberty, in the moral sense that Paine used it, has a shared common meaning, as expressed in the Declaration, and in the Articles.

"Freedom and rights mean a perfect equality of them," wrote Paine.

As he would later note, ten years later, about Madison's 1787 constitution, it is "an ill-advised attempt to replicate the British form of mixed constitution...their basis for justice becomes the balancing of particular class interests....they make it difficult for citizens to participate...it deprives citizens of private manners and public principles, and is driven by power and not consent, by coercive force and not the choices of citizens."

When Madison and Hamilton say, said Paine, 10 years later, that the central government needs more energy, "what they want is energy over the citizens. "A more perfect union," said Paine, about Madison's flawed arrangement, "meant a nominal nothing without principles."

And as noted earlier in the Introduction, Madison's nominal nothing, according to Arrows' Paradox, leads to endless cycling, over and over again, of the same problems in America. A more perfect union can mean anything, even the slavery of socialism, if the socialists gain control over the government, which in their logic of moral relativism, is perfectly logical.

Contrast Paine's statement in Common Sense, "let us hold out the hearty hand of friendship...an open and resolute friend, and a virtuous supporter of rights of mankind and of free and independent states of America," in a non-coercive constitution, with the coercive police powers of the state, in Madison's arrangement.

The perpetual class war of Madison's arrangement requires the coercive policy power to enforce citizen obedience, as demonstrated by Washington's use of the military power to quell the whiskey rebellion, and later, Shay's rebellion.

The phrase "mutual friendship" is lifted directly from Paine, and placed, by Thomas Burke, in the preamble of the Articles, as the basis of the new government. Burke's intent was "to secure and perpetuate mutual friendship and intercourse among the people of the different States in this union."

The Articles declare the purpose of the confederation is for the "States hereby severally to enter into a firm league of friendship with each other, for their common defense, the security of their liberties, and their mutual and general welfare, binding themselves to assist each other, against all force offered to, or attacks made upon them, or any of them, on account of religion, sovereignty, trade, or any other pretense whatever."

Burke believed that "the authority of the congress rested on the prior acts of the several states, to which the states gave their voluntary consent, and until those obligations were fulfilled, neither nullification of the authority of congress, exercising its due powers, nor secession from the compact itself was consistent with the terms of their original pledges."

According to Article XIII of the Confederation, any alteration of the Articles had to be approved unanimously. Of course, this is the basis of the moral transgression of the unconstitutional act committed by Madison and Hamilton in overthrowing the Articles in 1787.

Madison had no legal authority to overthrow the Articles. His state legislature had adopted the Articles, and Madison was a delegate to the General Assembly of Virginia, when the Articles were adopted.

As Burke wrote, "The Articles of this Confederation shall be inviolably observed by every State, and the Union shall be perpetual; nor shall any alteration at any time hereafter be made in any of them; unless such alteration be agreed to in a Congress of the United States, and be afterwards confirmed by the legislatures of every State."

Madison, and the Federalists who met in Philadelphia in 1787, knew that they intended to commit an immoral act in overthrowing the constitutional government of 1781, and they had known what they wanted to do, as early as 1777, with Dickson's first draft of the Articles.

The Federalists, and their most recent incarnation, were not then, and have never been, loyal patriots to the cause of American natural rights.

In Jefferson's philosophy of natural rights, the force that compels citizen obedience to the constitution is the shared commitment of the right to liberty. Jefferson wrote that "No one has a right to obstruct another exercising his faculties innocently for the relief of sensibilities made a part of his nature... the right to liberty is an all things equal guarantee of freedom of choice and action..."

Jefferson was addressing the issue Hobbes had raised about the force that would compel obedience after the authority of the Pope, and the authority of the King no longer compelled obedience. When Thomas Hobbes was writing The Leviathan, in the late 1640s, he had two earlier patterns of social authority to use as examples in developing his own model of civil authority.

Those two patterns of authority had coexisted for many years, and each had been undergoing a slow transformation, the outcome of which fascinated Hobbes. He raised the question of would replace either the King or the Church in performing the social function of holding dissociated individuals together in a cooperative society, and what force would compel obligation to serve the public purpose?

Jefferson answered Hobbes by stating that the force that creates obedience of the American citizens to obey the constitutional rules in a natural rights republic is the equal opportunity of upward occupational mobility. As long as every citizen has an opportunity to gain financial success, every citizen supports the equal freedom for any other citizen.

The cause of upward occupational mobility is economic growth that leads to a society of "self-made" citizens, who are not dependent on government for welfare. This connection between the purpose of the constitution and the functioning of the free market is the cause of liberty. The free market secures the liberty of the constitution.

According to Jefferson's natural rights philosophy, all human beings possess an original and inherent liberty which is inalienable. This liberty, explains Jefferson, is a liberty for the innocent actions of free citizens, that is, for actions that do not deprive others of their rights, or do not interfere with the realization of the community welfare.

The Declaration is a compact between citizens in each state to establish a rightful centralized political power, dedicated to protecting the natural rights of citizens that are left incompletely protected within each state government. The Declaration, and the Articles, moved the citizens of the United States toward an egalitarian individualism, with an appeal to natural rights.

Jefferson stated that the citizens in, "each state have an equal right to judge for itself as well as infractions as of the mode and measures of redress."

Morality in this natural rights republic is respect for the rights of others. Jefferson wrote that "the great and chief end of men's uniting into a commonwealth and putting themselves under government is the preservation of their property and rights."

Those rights were only secure, warned Jefferson, when the citizens accepted the principles that their natural rights were the gift of God.

The irreconcilable threat of global socialism in America is that the socialists do not believe in God, and do not support the egalitarianism of citizens in the natural rights republic. Just like the elites before them that Hobbes wrote about, the socialists do not believe in, or have faith in, the citizens to make their own best decisions about how to pursue their sovereign life path.

Jefferson felt compelled to write out the natural rights principles of government, in 1799, so that citizens could implement them, in the event that there was civil war between the Federalists and the common citizens.

Recall that at that time, Jefferson was running for President against John Adams, who had implemented the Alien and Sedition Acts to control the political activities of the anti-federalists. Jefferson was concerned that the social chaos of the civil war would erase the memory of his principles of government.

When Jefferson won the election of 1800, Federalists engaged in a massive effort to de-legitimize Jefferson's election, just as the Democrats and establishment Republicans today are attempting to undermine the government of President Trump.

In March of 1801, because of the impending threat of the Federalists, the nation came within one day of fighting the first American civil war.

Jefferson's natural rights principles were:
- Equality among citizens to participate in government.
- Privacy of citizens from the invasions of agents of government.
- The right to vote in free and fair elections.
- The protection of the natural and property rights of individuals as the supreme goal of government.

- Equal access to the courts and equality before the law.

Jefferson believed that individuals are rights-possessors, with the inalienable right to pursue their own happiness, manage their private lives, and be free of government coercion in their person and their property.

Jefferson wrote that subjugation, coercion, and manipulation arose when the participants to a political or constitutional exchange enter the political relationship with unequal economic power.

What Madison and Hamilton accomplished in overthrowing Jefferson's natural rights republic, was to re-institute the British class system of unequal economic power, built into the fabric of their constitution of 1787.

Madison's constitution essentially did away with monarchy and the heredity principle but replaced it with power in the hands of an oligarchic class, where the leading families acquired an unbalanced and unchecked political power.

Eventually, the elites in the Republican Party assumed this unbalanced political power to use the power of government to direct financial benefits to their own social class, and it is this unchecked power that would be so dangerous in the hands of the socialists.

The threat to individual freedom, from Jefferson's philosophy, occurs at the beginning of the constitutional exchange relationship, not in the welfare outcomes that result from the ensuing economic exchanges. This concern about the initial conditions of the constitution is the primary reason why Jefferson was so insistent on placing his metaphor of leaving the state of nature, where all citizens entered the new government under conditions of natural liberty and equality, into the Declaration.

"No one is born into moral subjugation to political power," stated Jefferson. When citizens leave nature to create their government, "all men are created equal... in nature all humans are equal... not subject to the rightful authority of any other human being... in a state of nature no rightful authority exists in nature. No man is subjected to the will or authority of any other man," he wrote, over and over again, from 1776, to the very last letter he wrote in 1826.

The threat to freedom in the natural rights republic arises because one party (the elites) have gained the initial illegitimate ability to subjugate the sovereign life path of the less powerful party (the non-elites). This unequal power exists in the constitution of 1787.

It would continue to exist under socialism.

The command and control regulations under socialism aim at correcting the unequal outcomes after the exchange has occurred, by attempting to manipulate incomes and prices through tax policies. In other words, the socialists accept the global monopoly power of corporations, and work to re-distribute income, without correcting the initial rules that give rise to unequal wealth.

The socialist regulations, taxation, and income transfers, however, leave the threat to freedom in place to re-occur generation after generation. Under Madison's scheme, the socialists have added the new feature that uses welfare payments of government to compel allegiance to the socialist party by making the citizens servile and dependent on government.

James Buchanan applies this concept of unequal constitutional power in, The Reason of Rules: Constitutional Political Economy, when he discusses the relationship between free markets and governmental power. He states that "…for most persons, the independence offered by the presence of market alternatives offers the maximal liberty possible."

When Buchanan discusses the question raised by Hobbes about the force that compels citizens to obey authority, he reaches the same conclusion that Thomas Paine, Thomas Jefferson, and Thomas Buchanan reached 200 years earlier. "No individual knows in advance where the individual may end up, given the choice between one set of constitutional rules or another," writes Buchanan.

In his book, Buchanan writes, "a rational individual, with a rational self-interest, would choose fair rules for all, aimed at the greatest freedom for all."

When citizens leave the state of nature, in constitutional decision-making under uncertainty, individuals would seek rules that had maximum equal rights for all, with special privileges for none. The end goal, or telos, of the constitution, in this case of rational self-interest, is individual freedom.

The teleos of global socialism is not individual freedom because socialists deny the existence of rational self-interest, in favor of multi-cultural logic, which suggests that the end goal of society is whatever the socialists say it is, at the precise moment that they say it. The collectivist constitution always ends in totalitarianism.

A collectivist society is always denying the individual the urge for this biologically defined sovereignty. In denying the creation of the mental image of the self in favor of the collectivist image of the individual, the collectivist culture disrupts the brain's interplay between internal images and external truth values.

Rawls, in Justice as Fairness, proposed that fairness requires no collective decision that did not improve the distribution of wealth to the least advantaged members.

The natural rights alternative of fairness suggests that no process of exchange, either by majority voting of citizens or through the price mechanism of the market, can be fair if it involves subjugation, coercion, and manipulation of one's fate.

The public purpose in the natural rights republic is served by constitutional rules that promote common external values of trust, fair dealing, truthful representations, and promise keeping.

Cooperation between individuals occurs when the individuals assume, prior to entering into the exchange process, that these common values are influencing the interpretation of truth the same way, in both citizens to an exchange.

These are the values expressed by Jefferson in the Declaration, and by Thomas Buchanan, in his re-draft of the Articles.

In the natual rights individualist society, the moral freedom of the individual involves the decreasing reliance on externally imposed standards of behavior and ethical values regarding the treatment of others in civil exchanges. Moral development of the individual occurs during life through an increasing reliance on internalized mental values that address the welfare of others.

When Madison and Hamilton suggested that only the virtuous elite possessed these moral values, they denied the moral foundation of Jefferson's natural rights republic.

In the natural rights individualist society, the role of government is to reduce the chance situations that other individuals or the police power of the state will be used to override the individual's freedoms of choice in pursuing their sovereign life mission. The government serves this function by administering the constitutional framework of collective decision making whose goal is to secure just outcomes to the laws that individuals give to themselves.

Government, and the pursuit of just outcomes, in the natural rights republic, is a process of collective decision-making, not an outcome.

For socialists, government and fairness is an outcome, achieved only by the elite socialists using the police power of the state to enforce their ideas of fairness in outcomes.

The point is that justice in the natural rights democracy depends on the initial adoption of a unique set of moral values to insure social stability. Whether this unique constellation of cultural values is widespread and commonly held throughout the society is contingent upon the process of social consensus about the moral values of truth, and fair honest dealings, when citizens leave the state of nature.

The logic of the natural rights republic, in other words, is that the biological function of the individual brain provides the rationale for why and how society should define the public purpose in terms of improving individual welfare.

A shared set of constitutional values about trust within a culture strengthens the degree of social cohesion and cooperation. The shared values makes it more likely that individual brains will be sorting and selecting images based upon the coherence between internal models and external images during the course of an exchange.

In re-imposing the British social class system, in 1787, Madison denied the possibility that America would ever have a common set of constitutional moral values, because he thought that the purpose of government was to balance one class against the other.

In other words, Madison's flawed arrangement unleashed perpetual class warfare in America, exactly as citizens see today with the rhetoric of the socialists. Jefferson's constitutional arrangement was based upon common moral values. Madison's constitution was not.

As a result, American citizens have endured perpetual class warfare, and a dysfunctional economy, based upon speculation by the financial elites, that collapses every 10 years or so.

About 100 years after the adoption and ratification of the Madison's constitution, during one of America's more spectacular economic collapses, the agrarian leader, Tom Watson asked in his newspaper, "What is Labor's Fair Share?"

A better question may have been "What are Fair Constitutional Rules for Labor?"

The constitutional rules that made life miserable for the farmers in 1887, had been created by Madison and Hamilton, in 1787, to achieve separation of powers in the branches of government, the indirect election of representatives, and judicial review of legislation, all intended to bury any incipient tendencies to a popular citizen's democratic government

The populists of 1887 learned a hard lesson that hard work, by itself, does not insure financial success or lead to upward occupational mobility in America. The farmers had the right set of values about work and society, but the wrong strategy.

Leonidas Polk, the agrarian leader who founded N. C. State University, said "Labor is thus associated in our mind with all that is honorable in birth, refined in manners, bright in intellect, manly in character and magnanimous in soul."

For the populists, hard work was associated with the value of independence and the moral value of a person. In the Savage Ideal, Bruce Clayton notes that in the South, "work was a moral absolute, an outer sign of inner worth..."

For farmers, not being dependent on others was the outer sign of moral worth.

The values of the farmers, in 1887, were based upon their correct interpretation of the moral values proclaimed by Jefferson, in the Declaration, that the farmers were entitled to the value that they produced from their work, under fair rules of exchange.

"But, what is a slave?" asked a New Jersey patriot in 1765, "but one who depends upon the will of another for the enjoyment of his life and property." Dependency, in the minds of farmers was equated with slavery, and slavery in the American moral setting would be avoided by hard work and fair rules of exchange.

The farmers kept trying to work within the existing two party political system to reform the political process and did not recognize that Madison's constitutional rules had rigged the political system against the non-elites.

No set of policy reforms would ever overcome the flaws of an unbalanced and unfair set of constitutional rules that operated within the social class system built by Madison.

As Charles Beard argued in his 1913 book, An Economic Interpretation of the Constitution of the United States, Madison assumed that commercial and financial interests were the primary forces that needed to be balanced against the non-elite social classes, in the three branches of government.

Beard showed that the Founding Federalists all had a personal vested financial interest in skewing the results of the new constitutional rules to suit their own needs, while at the same time, attempting to ensure stability in the government by establishing rules of procedure that balanced financial factions against each other.

Stability, used in this sense means perpetual constitutional rules that can never be revoked, even when it becomes obvious that the rules are destructive of the ends that they were intended to achieve.

Madison stated in Federalist 10, "The most common and durable sources of factions has been the various and unequal distribution of property…creditors, debtors, landed interests, manufacturing interests mercantile interests, a moneyed interest."

Madison argued that, " …the real threats to rights in a republic lay not in arbitrary acts of government misruling its people but in the more disturbing possibility that popular majorities,(non-elites), acting through government, would willfully trample on the rights of individuals and minorities," (the well born).

If the three branches of government could be kept distinct and separate, and the geographic sphere of representation could be extended, Madison argued, then the threat of democratic tyranny would be lessened.

On the other hand, Madison feared that if the non-elite democratic forces at the state level ever achieved unified power over all three branches, at the national level at any one time, the central government would collapse into a democratic tyranny.

As Hamilton explained, "Every community divides itself into hostile interests of the few and the many, the rich and well-born against the mass of people If either of these interests possessed all the power it would oppress the other…we (the well born) need to be rescued from the democracy."

Hamilton's favorite term of endearment for the non-elites was "the howling masses."

Or, as James Dickson stated at the convention in 1787, the new constitution must protect "the worthy against the licentious."

While keeping these various factions separate in the new aristocratic republic, Madison was also concerned that the democratic majority not disrupt the flow of financial benefits to the propertied minority.

Madison shared the opinion of Jonathan Jackson that the main threat of tyranny originated in the excesses of democracy at the state level.

In his 1788 book, Thoughts Upon The Political Situation in the United States, Jackson wrote, "A natural aristocracy that had to dominate public authority in order to prevent America from degenerating into a democratic licentiousness, into a government where the people would be directed by no rule but their own will and caprice...Tyranny by the people was the worst kind because it left few resources to the oppressed (the elites)."

The farmers, in western Pennsylvania, in 1792, had been trying to pay their taxes in paper money, not in gold and silver, as preferred by the elites who owned government bonds. Payment of taxes and debt repayment in paper money was "oppressive."

"Oppressed" in this Federalist usage meant the oppression of the well born by the licentious non-elites, who were using state government to re-write laws on credit and debt payment.

John Dickson explained that Madison's new Federal constitution placed the remedy in the hands (well born) which feel the disorder of democracy, whereas the antifederalists placed the remedy in the hands of citizens (the common people), who cause the disorder, by not paying their taxes and debts in gold and silver.

Madison took away the farmer's ability to pay their taxes in paper money, issued by the states. Madison, in Article 1, Section 10, centralized the power of the federal government on debt repayment, at the state level, by eliminating the power of the states to regulate debt contracts,.

In setting up his centralized power, Madison did not anticipate that socialists, in 2008, would gain control over the aristocratic reins of government that he had created.

The same power that subjugated the farmers in 1887 can easily be used today by the socialists in order to subjugate non-socialists to a borderless global government, operating outside the jurisdiction of the national borders.

Global socialism, as a unifying ideology, is not a commercial or financial "faction" in the sense that Madison used the term. It is, however, a subversive force that can capture all three branches of government, at one time.

The political problem that Madison left America with was that his constitutional system eliminated the ability of non-elite classes to reclaim the government from the socialists.

As Gordon Wood has pointed out, in The Creation of the American Republic, not only did Madison's scheme provide for a system dominated by "...natural leaders who knew better than the people as a whole what was good for society," but it also succeeded in removing the non-natural leaders from the political process."

Wood noted, "In fact, the people did not actually participate in government any more...The American (Federalists) had taken the people out of the government altogether.

The true distinction of the American system, wrote Madison in Federalist 71, "lies in the total exclusion of the people, in their collective capacity in any share in the government."

As soon as Madison's constitution was published, Mason stated on September 15, 1787 that the plan of amendments was exceptionable and dangerous. He stated, "As the proposing of amendments is in both modes to depend in the first immediately and in the second ultimately on Congress, no amendments of the proper kind would ever be obtained by the people, if the Government should become oppressive."

Mason went on to say that Americans had been duly warned about the incipient aristocratic tyranny. "These gentlemen who will be elected senators, will fix themselves in the federal town, and become citizens of that town more than of your state."

"This government will commence in a moderate aristocracy," Mason said. "It is at present impossible to foresee whether it will, in its operation, produce a monarchy or a corrupt, oppressive aristocracy, it will most probably vitiate some years between the two, and then terminate in the one or the other."

Mason thought that Madison's government would terminate, in an oppressive aristocracy, and did not foresee that the government would end in a corrupt socialist dictatorship.

Mason was accurate, however, in his prediction about the Federalists.

Less than 5 years later, Hamilton had created an oppressive aristocracy, and led an army of 13,000 federal soldiers into western Pennsylvania, in 1792, to crush the farmers who refused to pay their excise taxes in gold and silver.

There was no gold and silver in circulation for the farmers to pay their taxes. And, when the farmers did not pay their taxes in gold and silver, the Federalist tax collectors came and took their farm lands, and gave the lands to the aristocrats, in payment of debt on government bonds.

One hundred years later, when the farmers of 1887 did not repay their debts to the merchant's on a timely basis, the government agents came and took their farm lands. This later strategy of taking the land away from the farmers was called the "debt-lien" system, all perfectly legal under the constitutional rules established by Madison.

Hamilton did see the benefits of this constitutional arrangement for the elites, as he noted, that "all parts of society were of a piece, that all ranks and degrees were organically connected through a great chain in such a way that those on top were necessarily involved in the welfare of those below them."

The intractable political problem Madison left the nation is that when the Republicans abdicated their historic mission of protecting the social class rights of the natural aristocracy, there were no rules identified in Madison's constitution to "alter or abolish" the incipient socialist tyranny.

There are today, as there were in 1787, only two political parties, one now a global socialist Democrat party, and the other now a globalist Republican party.

In other words, as bad as Madison's two party arrangement was, at least it identified the national sovereign interest as the legitimate sphere of interest of the central government.

Both parties have abandoned the national sovereign interest, in favor of their new globalist goals. In America, there can only be two political parties, one that was supposed to represent the elites, and one that was supposed to represent the non-elites. Those historic roles have been eradicated.

Voting for representatives of a globalist government does not represent a legitimate choice for citizens. The way that Madison wrote the election laws for the House and Senate made his two party political arrangement irrevocable.

Madison unleashed a perpetual class war in America between the elites and the non-elites that is still a class war, but it is now a class war in a global setting.

No amount of reform of the Democrat Party, in 1887, by the farmers, and no amount of wishful thinking today, that the Republican Party may somehow morph into a credible conservative party, will change Madison's two party arrangement.

What Madison overthrew, in 1787, was the voluntary economy of exchange of the Articles of Confederation, where common citizens could freely gain the value of their labor (property).

Madison replaced the Articles, based upon equal commercial exchanges, with government rules, where the elites dominated the terms of exchange with their unbalanced, and unchecked government power.

The aristocratic American government created by Madison was stable as long as the Republicans (the well born), created economic growth. After 1992, when the American economy no longer experienced economic growth, citizens became susceptible to the propaganda of socialism.

To answer Tom Watson's question, obtaining labor's fair share today means creating better constitutional rules for the fair distribution of income, by restoring the moral values of the natural rights republic.

Fair distribution occurs as a result of the moral values at the beginning of the constitutional exchange, not after the exchange has occurred.

Madison's flaw was his deliberate omission that the ultimate goal of the constitution was protecting individual freedoms. This flaw of omitting the end goal results in a dysfunctional government that is commonly described as the "Arrow Paradox."

Some American historians celebrate Madison's flaw of leaving out the purpose of the constitution as being evidence of the genius of the mind of the founder. Benjamin Barber, for example, cites this flaw as the virtue of American "public purposelessness."

Paine's term for the same idea was a "nominal nothing."

In the mid-1990s, the U. S. Central Bank, in addition to the Republicans, also became disconnected from the sovereign national interests of common citizens. Just like the Republicans, the Fed's new allegiance was to a borderless, global economy, operated for the benefit of the world's financial elites.

The way out of this globalist conundrum is to restore a version of the Articles of Confederation in Jefferson's natural rights republic.

The rules are aimed at a fair system of exchange where society is made up of self-made citizens, who are not slaves to the government.

The solution of the Arrow's paradox is to assume in the preamble of the new constitution, that only individual's have a welfare function, and to require that the constitution contain an explicit statement of the ultimate goal to be achieved via the constitutional rules.

For example, a better natural rights constitutional preamble could state:

We, the People of the United States, in Order to protect the natural rights of citizens, establish equal Justice before the law for all, prohibit special interests derived from government, insure domestic Tranquility, provide for the common defense, and secure the Blessings of Liberty to ourselves and our Posterity, do ordain and establish this Constitution for the United States of America.

In The Reason of Rules, Buchanan and Brennan write that "Our specific claim is that justice takes its meaning from the rules for the social order within which notions of justice are to be applied. To appeal to considerations of justice is to appeal to relevant rules."

No individual, in the natural rights constitution, knows in advance where that individual may end up, given the choice between one set of constitutional rules or another. A rational individual, with a rational self-interest, would choose fair rules for all, aimed at the greatest freedom for all.

In constitutional decision-making under uncertainty, individuals would seek rules that had maximum equal rights for all, with special privileges for none. The end goal, or telos, of the natural rights constitution, given the initial assumption of rational self-interest, is individual freedom.

This interpretation of justice as fair rules is dramatically different than the Rawlsian notion of fairness that relies on a set of elites who judge the fairness of welfare outcomes and have the power to shift income from one social group to another.

Of course, the socialists start out with the initial assumption that individuals do not have a rational self-interest, and that only the socialist elites can determine what is in the best interests of any individual, who is defined by the socialists as a cog in a collectivist social group (feminists, gays, blacks, poor people, etc.).

Buchanan argues that the issue of economic fairness must be determined through the process of making and enforcing fair constitutional rules, not on manipulating welfare outcomes.

Attempts to define a group social welfare function, and then to maximize that function, will always violate Arrow's condition of non-dictatorship.

As Buchanan has pointed out, that social welfare function contains variables that promote the welfare of the politicians and bureaucrats who created it. The welfare function they maximize turns out to be their own. If it is not subjected to sunset or recall, the bureaucracy becomes a permanent feature of the political environment.

Fair Rules of Citizen Consent
In the natural rights republic, the origin of constitutional political authority is the consent of the governed. Citizens agree to voluntarily obey the constitution for the legislative laws that they make and give to themselves.

For example:
> That all power is vested in, and consequently derived from, the people; that magistrates are their trustees and servants, and at all times amenable to them.
> That government is, or ought to be, instituted for the common benefit, protection and security of the people, nation or community; and not for the particular emolument or advantage of any single man, family, or soft of men, who are a part only of that community, And that the community hath an indubitable, unalienable and indefeasible right to reform, alter, or abolish government in such manner as shall be by that community judged most conducive to the public weal.
> But no part of a citizen's property can be justly taken from him, or applied to public uses, without his own consent, or that of his legal representatives: Nor can any man who is conscientiously scrupulous of bearing arms, be justly compelled thereto, if he will pay such equivalent, nor are the people bound by any laws, but such as they have in like manner assented to, for their common good.
> As every citizen may preserve his independence, (if without a sufficient estate) ought to have some profession, calling, trade or farm, whereby he may honestly subsist, there can be no necessity for, nor use in establishing offices of profit, the usual effects of which are dependence and servility unbecoming freemen, in the possessors and expectants; faction, contention, corruption, and disorder among the people.

No citizen, nor corporation or association of citizens have any other title to obtain advantages, or particular and exclusive privileges distinct from those of the community, than what rises from the consideration of services rendered to the public, and this title being in nature neither hereditary nor transmissible to children or descendants or relations by blood; the idea of a citizen born into an estates as a magistrate, lawgiver, or judge is absurd and unnatural.

In order to prevent those elected representatives to the national government who are vested with elected or delegated authority from becoming oppressors, the citizens, acting through their state governments, have a right at such periods and in such manner as they shall establish by their frame of state government, to cause their public officers to return to private life; and to fill up vacant places by certain and regular elections and appointments.

And that the citizens have an indubitable, unalienable and indefeasible right to reform, alter, or abolish the government in such manner as shall be judged most conducive to the public weal.

Fair Rules for Federal Elections

Election of one U. S. Senator, per state, whose constitutional mission is to protect the interests of citizens in their states from the threat of tyranny of the central government.

Establishing House election districts by quantitative criteria, for periods of 10 years.

Constitutional procedures for establishing voter qualifications and voting procedures.

The delegation to each State Secretary of State the authority by Congress to form state election commission to oversee integrity of voter registration and voting process in each federal election.

The right of citizens in each state to recall federal elected representatives by vote of the registered members of the parties that elected them.

An oath of allegiance of newly elected representatives to defend the constitution and the rights of citizens as expressed in the Declaration of Independence.

Fair Rules on Representation

Term of office and term limits of senators. Senators serve four year terms and may succeed in office once, and no more than 10 years in a lifetime.

Term of office and term limits for all House of Representatives. Two year terms, 4 terms total and no more than 10 years in a lifetime.

Limits on Congress on bills enacted under the necessary and proper clause to only "expressly" enumerated actions that defend natural rights from the government.

That each bill contain a preamble that justifies the enactment as necessary and proper.

For Example:

That the people have a right to uniform government; and, therefore, that no bill or tax whose interests are outside the sovereign interests of the United States, or separate from, or independent of the government of the United States, ought to be enacted.

And before any law be made for raising taxes, the purpose for which any tax is to be raised ought to appear clearly to the preamble of the legislation stating the constitutional integrity of the tax.

Fair Rules on the Function of Federal Government
Term limits of 10 years for all government employees and congressional staff. Money and tax bills originate in the House, and are voted on by the Senate. Bright line rules for impeachment of elected federal representatives, or appointed officials, initiated by either the federal government, or in the legislatures of the states.

Constitutional restrictions of the domain of power of the Federal Reserve to the exclusive benefit of U. S. citizens and the operation of the U. S. domestic economy.

Constitutional limits on the issuance of federal debt and a constitutional requirement that the
U. S. Department of the Treasury limit the national debt ceiling to a target debt level in any 10 year period, by approval of a majority of state legislatures.

Fair Rules of Justice
Elimination of lifetime tenure for all U. S federal judges, including the Supreme Court, with appointment for 10 year periods, with no right of reappointment. Bright line constitutional rules Congressional impeachment of federal judges for infidelity to the constitution.

Judicial review of federal issues restricted to a clause or power enumerated or granted in the constitution to the federal government.

Judicial review of issues originating in states restricted to violations of natural and civil rights.

Judicial review restricted to issues related to state laws on interstate commerce.

Rules on States Rights and Federalism

The states are the contracting parties that form the constitutional contract.

For example:
> (From the Articles of Confederation) "The said States hereby severally enter into a firm league of friendship with each other, for their common defense, the security of their liberties, and their mutual and general welfare, binding themselves to assist each other, against all force offered to, or attacks made upon them, or any of them, on account of religion, sovereignty, trade, or any other pretense whatever."

Senate selects 7 members of the Council of States to provide policy advice for the president on issues arising between the states and the national government.

The right of states to leave the union.

For example:
> That all citizens have a natural inherent right to emigrate from one state to another that will receive them, or to form a new state in vacant countries, or in such countries as they can purchase, whenever they think that thereby they may promote their own happiness.

The right of new states to be admitted to the Union by Congress.
State citizen reunion ratification every ten years.

Constitutional procedures for state legislatures to alter or abolish the central government, when the central government becomes destructive of citizen rights.

Amendments to the constitution initiated either at the U. S. Congressional level or initiated by a 60% super majority of state legislatures.

Constitutional prohibition of the use of the U. S. military against the citizens of any state, and empowerment of state militias to protect and defend citizens against the federal military.

The right of citizens to bear arms and cross state lines armed, with immunity.

Constitutional Rules for Political Parties

Parties select candidates for office in August for federal election held in last weekend of October.

Voter ID cards issued by party for registered members of the party.

Parties obligated to prepare statement of principles of party and issues of election.

Candidates for each party swear and affirm an oath to defend the stated principles of the party, if elected.

Right to recall elected representatives of that party limited by registered members of the Party.

Political parties registered by State Secretary of State, as non-profit corporations.

Political parties certified by State Secretary of State by valid petition signed by registered members of the party equal to 10% of all registered voters in the state.

Parties de-certified by Secretary of State in any federal presidential election where the total votes cast by registered members for President is less than 10%.

Secretary of State issues voter ID card for all non-affiliated registered voters.

Fair Rules of Economic Exchange

That national social welfare in this constitution is a function of individual welfare and that the individual citizen knows what is in the best interest of that citizen to improve the life, welfare and happiness of the individual.

That citizens are entitled to the rights of reward for their work.

That the economic welfare of the nation is improved when all citizens work and have an equal opportunity for upward occupational mobility.

That the economic welfare of the nation is improved when all citizens contribute taxes to the maintenance and operation of the Federal government.

For example:

> That every citizen has a right to be protected in the enjoyment of life, liberty and property, and therefore is bound to contribute his proportion towards the expense of that protection, and yield his personal service when necessary. But no part of a citizen's property can be justly taken from him, or applied to public uses, without his own consent, or that of his legal representatives.

That the greatest freedom and independence for citizens is offered by the operation of the free and competitive market and that the economy authorized to operate under this government is based upon the principles of free competitive markets.

That all treaties of foreign trade be demonstrated to improve the lives and welfare of the individual citizens.

Conclusion.

With the advent of a global socialist ideology in the Democrat Party, the nation has entered into new unchartered territory.

Madison's constitutional arrangement was designed to pit the elite special financial interests in one political social class against the non-elites in the other party. He made the constitutional rules unbalanced and unfair, to benefit the financial elites.

The socialists are poised and positioned to obtain the levers of power that had been reserved for the financial elites.

At the same moment in history that the Democrats abandoned their allegiance to the middle class, the Republicans morphed into a global corporatist party, which no longer defends American sovereignty.

As a consequence of these two political developments, the citizens of America do not have a legitimate choice for a party to represent their interests.

Citizens under Madison's constitution did well when they had economic and financial opportunities for wealth and upward occupational mobility, and they have not had these conditions since the Republicans passed laws that severely damaged the welfare of the citizens.

In the absence of economic growth, citizens have needlessly suffered economic failure and depressions.

This book described the economic consequences of the Republican abdication of their historical role.
- The Disastrous Macro Economic Consequences of Republican Trade Policies.
- The Negative Consequence of the Republican Trade Policies on Job Creation.
- The Consequence of the Republican Abdication On American Ingenuity and Technological Innovation.
- The Consequences of the Republican Economic Policies on New Venture Creation and Entrepreneurship.
- Regional Economic Decline Caused By The Republican Abdication.

The book described that future politics in America had to come up with policies on how to manage the relationship between a new American Natural Rights Republic and 1500 American global corporations.

The constitution of the new natural rights republic is based upon Jefferson's principles of natural rights:
- Equality among citizens to participate in government.
- Privacy of citizens from the invasions of agents of government.
- The right to vote in free and fair elections.
- The protection of the natural and property rights of individuals as the supreme goal of government.
- Equal access to the courts and equality before the law.

Restoring the American natural rights republic means the citizens have two major tasks ahead of them:

1. The citizens must eliminate the socialist threat to freedom. The next book in this series explains that if, and when, California citizens vote to leave the Union to form their own socialist state, that socialists in other states should be encouraged to emigrate to California.
2. After the socialist threat has been eliminated, citizens in the remaining states need to hold a constitutional convention and re-write fair constitutional rules.

Bibliography

Adams, John, The Political Writings of John Adams: Representative Selections, Edited with
an Introduction by George A. Peek, Jr., Liberal Arts Press, New York, 1954.

Arrow, Kenneth Joseph, Social Choice and Individual Values, Wiley, New York, 1951.

Ayers, Edward L., The Promise of the New South: Life After Reconstruction, Oxford University Press, New York, 1992.

Abramovitz, M. and David, Paul, "Convergence and Deferred Catch-Up: Productivity and the Waning American Exceptionalism," in Landau, Ralph, Taylor, Timothy and Wright, Gavin, (editors), The Mosaic of Economic Growth, Stanford University Press, Stanford, 1996.

Acs, Zoltan, Regional Innovation, Knowledge and Global Change, Pinter, London, 2000.

Aghion, Philippe and Howitt, Peter, Endogenous Growth Theory, MIT Press, Cambridge, 1998.

Alderman Neil, "Local Product Development Trajectories: Engineering Establishments in Three Contrasting Regions," in Malecki E.J. and Oinas P. (Editors), Making Connections: Technological Learning and Regional Economic Change, Aldershot, Ashgate, 1999.

Allen, J., "Information Systems Use In Continuously Innovative Organizations," in Larsen, Tors, and McGuire, Eugene, (Editors), Information Systems Innovation and Diffusion: Issues and Directions, Idea Group Publishing, Hershey, 1998.

Appleby, Joyce, Capitalism and a New Social Order, 1984

Arrow, Kenneth, Social Choice and Individual Values, John Wiley & Sons, Inc., New York, 1963.

Bailyn, Bernard, The Ideological Origins of the American Revolution, Belnap Press Cambridge, 1967.

Beard, Charles, An Economic Interpretation of the Constitution of the United States, MacMillan Co, NY, 1913.

Belenzon Sharon and Schankerman. Mark, The Impact of Private Ownership, Incentives and Local Development Objectives on University Technology Transfer Performance, CEP Discussion Paper No. 779, September 2007.

Bell, M., and Pavitt, K., cited in Globalization, Information Technology and Development, J. James, MacMillan Press, London, 1999.

Bertuglia, C. et al., "An Interpretive Survey of Innovative Behavior and Diffusion," in Bertuglia, Cristoforo, Lombardo, Silvana, and Nijkamp, Peter, Innovative Behavior In Space and Time, Springer, Berlin, 1997.

Best, Michael, The New Competition: Institutions of Industrial Restructuring, Harvard University Press, Cambridge, 1990.

Blau, Peter Michael, Exchange and Power in Social Life, J. Wiley, New York, 1964.

Blaug, Mark, Economic History and the History of Economics, New York University Press, New York, 1986.

Boland, R. and Tenkasi, R., "Perspective Making and Perspective Taking In Communities of Knowing," in. DeSanctis, G., and. Fulk, J., (editors), Shaping Organizational Form: Communication, Connection and Community, Sage Public, Thousand Oaks, Ca., 1996.

Bradford, Scott, Grieco, Paul, and Hufbauer, Gary, "Trading Barbs: A Primer on the Globalization Debate," The Regional Economist, October 2007.

Brennan, Geoffrey, and Buchanan, James M., The Reason of Rules: Constitutional Political
Economy, Cambridge University Press, Cambridge, New York, 1985.

Bruno, A. and Tyebjee, J., "The Environment For Entrepreneurship," in Kent, Calvin, Sexton, Donald, and Vesper, Karl, (editors), Encyclopedia of Entrepreneurship, Prentice-Hall, Inc., Englewood Cliffs, 1982.

Buchanan, James M., Constitutional Economics, Blackwell,Oxford, UK., Cambridge, Mass.,
1991.

Buchanan, James M., Theory of Public Choice: Political Applications of Economics, University of Michigan Press, Ann Arbor, 1972.

Buderi, R., "Lucent Ventures Into The Future," Technology Review, November-December, 2000.

Calvin, W., The Cerebral Symphony: Seashore Reflections on The Structure of Consciousness, Bantam Books, New York, 1990.

Cantwell, J., "The Globalization of Technology: What Remains of the Product Cycle Model," in Archibugi, Daniele, and Michie, Jonathan, Technology, Globalisation and Economic Performance, Cambridge University Press, Cambridge, 1997.

Carlsson, B., "Technological Systems and Economic Development Potential: Four Swedish Case Studies," in Shionoya, Yuichi, and Perlman, Mark, Innovation In Technology, Industry and Institutions: Studies In Schumpeterian Perspectives, University of Michigan Press, Ann Arbor, 1994.

Carter, A. P., "A Linear Programming System Analyzing Embedded Technological Change," Kurtz, Heinz, D., (editor), et. al , Input-Output Analysis, Volume I, Edward Elgar, Cheltenham, 1998.

Cash, W. J. (Wilbur Joseph), The Mind of the South: 1900-1941, 1st ed., Alfred A. Knopf, New York, 1941.

Chandler, Alfred, D. Jr., and Mazlish, Bruce, (editors), Leviathans: Multinational Corporations and the New Global History, Cambridge University Press, Cambridge, 2005.

Christensen, Clayton, and Raynor, Michael, The Innovator's Solution: Creating and Sustaining Successful Growth, Harvard Business School Press, Boston, 2003.

Christensen, Clayton, M., "The Rules of Innovation," Technology Review, June 2002.

Christensen, Clayton, M., Anthony, Scott, D., and Roth, Erik, Seeing What's Next: Using The Theories of Innovation To Predict Industry Change, Harvard Business School Press, Boston, 2004.

Cornell, Saul, The Other Founders, UNC Press, Chapel Hill, 1999.

Coombs, R., Saviotti, P. and Walsh, V. Economics and Technological Change, Rowman and Littlefield, Totowa, NJ, 1987.

Czamanski, Stan, Regional Science Techniques In Practice: The Case of Nova Scotia, D. C. Heath and Company, Lexington, 1972.

DeSanctis, G., and Fulk, J., Shaping Organizational Form: Communication, Connection and Community, Sage Publications, Thousand Oaks, Ca., 1999.

DeSoto, Hernando, The Mystery of Capital: Why Capitalism Triumphs in the West and Fails Everywhere Else, Basic Books, New York, 2000.

Donnellon, A., and. Scully, M., "A Teams Performance and Rewards: Will Post-Bureaucratic Organization Be A Post-Meritocratic Organization?" in Hechscher, C., and Donnellon, A., (editors), The Post-Bureaucratic Organization: New Perspectives on Organizational Change, Sage Publications, Thousand Oaks, Ca.,1994.

Duchin, Faye, "An Input-Output Approach to Analyzing the Future Economic Implications of Technological Change," in Miller, Ronald, and Polenske, Karen, Frontiers of Input-Output Analysis, Oxford University Press, New York, 1989.

Duchin, Faye, Structural Economics: Measuring Change In Technology, Lifestyles and The Environment, Island Press, Washington, 1998.

Duchin, Faye, and Szyld, D. B., "A Dynamic I-O Model With Assured Positive Output," in Input-Output Analysis, Volume I, Kurtz, Henry, (Editor), et. al., Edward Elgar, Cheltenham, 1998.

Evans, P. and Wurster, T., Blown to Bits: How The New Economics of Information Transforms Strategy, Harvard University Press, Boston, 2000.

Feldman, M. P., and Kutay, A. S., "Innovation and Strategy in Space: Towards a Location Theory of the Firm," in Bertuglia, Cristoforo, Lombardo, Silvana, and Nijkamp, Peter, Innovative Behavior In Space and Time, Springer, Berlin, 1997.

Feser, Edward, J., Globalization, Regional Economic Policy and Research, Department of Urban and Regional Planning, University of Illinois, Urbana-Champaign, 2005.

Feser, Edward, J., "Enterprises, External Economies and Economic Development," Journal of Planning Literature, (Vol 12 #3), February 1998.

Feser, Edward, J., Old and New Theories of Industry Clusters, Department of Urban and Regional Planning, University of Illinois, Urbana- Champaign, 1998.

Fifarek, Brian, Veloso, Francisco and Davidson, Cliff, "Offshoring Technology Innovation: A Case Study of Rare-earth Technology,"Journal of Operations Management Volume 26, Issue 2, March 2008.

Fischer, Manfred, "Innovation, Knowledge Creation and Systems of Innovation," The Annals of Regional Science, (Vol. 35 #2), 2001.

Fleming, S., "Capitalization and Finance: The View From Georgia," Southern Growth, Summer, 1996.

Frank, Thomas, Listen Liberal: Or, Whatever Happened to the Party of the People, Scribe Publication, London, 2016

Gaylereps-Gres,, A Dynamic Perspective on Next-Generation Offshoring: The Global Sourcing of Science and Engineering Talent, Academy of Management, 2008.

Goddard, J.B. et al., "The Impact of New Information Technology on Urban and Regional Structure in Europe," in Thwaites, A. T., and Oakley, R. P., (editors), The Regional Economic Impact of Technological Change, St. Martin's Press, New York, 1985.

Goddard, J. B. and Richardson, R., "Why Geography Will Still Matter: What Jobs Go Where?" in Dutton, W., (editor), Information and Communication Technologies: Visions and Realities, Oxford University Press, Oxford, 1996.

Goodman, B., "Lucent's Self-Inflicted Wounds Aren't Fatal," Red Herring, October 30, 2000.

Goralski, W. and Kolon, M., IP Telephony, McGraw-Hill, New York, 2000.

Greider, William, "A New Giant Sucking Sound," The Nation, December 13, 2001.

Haley, Usha, C., Multinational Corporations In Political Environments: Ethics, Values and Strategies, World Scientific Publishing, Singapore, 2001.

Haltiwanger, John, Ron Jarmin, and Javier Miranda. "Business Formation and Dynamics by Business Age: Results from the New Business Dynamics Statistics." Presented at the Comparative Analysis of Enterprise (Micro) Data Conference, Budapest, Hungary. 2008.

Hamilton, Alexander, Madison, James, and Jay, John, The Federalist: A Collection of Essays Written in Favor of the New Constitution as Agreed Upon by the Federal Convention, September September 17, 1787, Reprinted from the original text under the editorial supervision of Henry B. Dawson. Essays written by Alexander Hamilton, James Madison and John Jay under pseudonym of "Publius".

Hanusch, Horst, Evolutionary Economics: Applications of Schumpeter's Ideas, Cambridge University Press, Cambridge, 1988.

Heertje, A.,"Schumpeter and Technical Change," in Hanusch, Horst, Evolutionary Economics: Applications of Schumpeter's Ideas, Cambridge University Press, Cambridge, 1988.

Hempel, C., "Ericsson Workers Fearing Job Cuts," Raleigh News and Observer, October, 2000.

Hicks, J. R., Value and Capital, Clarendon Press, Oxford, 1939.

Hira, Ron and Hira, Anil, Outsourcing America: What's Behind Our National Crisis and How We Can Reclaim American Jobs, AMACOM, 2005.

Hoffert, Robert, A Politics of Tensions: The Articles of Confederation and American Political Ideas, University Press of Colorado 1992

Holton, Woody, Unruly Americans and the Origins of the Constitution, Hill and Wang, NY, 2007.

Horowitz, I. L., Power, Politics and People: The Collected Essays of C. Wright Mills, Oxford University Press, New York, 1967.

Horwitz, Robert, The Moral Foundations of the American Revolution, 1986

Hunt, E. K., History of Economic Thought: Critical Perspective, Harper Collins, New York, 1992.

Hymer, Stephen. H., (dissertation of 1960, published 1976), The International Operations of National Firms: A Study of Direct Foreign Investment, MIT Press, Cambridge, 1976.

Jacobs, Jane, Cities and the Wealth of Nations: Principles of Economic Life, Random House, New York, 1984.

Jaffe. A., "Technological Opportunity and Spillovers of R & D: Evidence From Firm's Patents, Profits, and Market Value," American Economic Review 76, #5, 1986.

James, M.J., Globalization, Information Technology and Development, MacMillan Press, London, 1999.

Jensen, Merrill, The Articles of Confederation, University of Wisconsin Press, Madison, 1970.

Jones, Geoffrey, Multinational and Global Capitalism: From The Nineteenth to the Twenty-First Century, Oxford University Press, Oxford, 2005.

Kindleberger, Charles, P., World Economic Primacy: 1500 to 1990. Oxford University Press, New York, 1996.

Kobrin, Stephen, Multinational Corporations, the Protest Movement and the Future of Global: Our Resistance Is As Global As Your Oppression, Meeting of the International Studies Association in Chicago, 2001.

Korten, David, When Corporations Rule The World, Second Edition, Kumerian Press, Inc. Bloomfield, Conn., 2001.

Krugman, Paul, Pop Internationalism, MIT Press, Cambridge, 1996.

Kuznets, S., Secular Movements In Production and Prices, Houghton, Mifflin, Boston, 1930.

Landes, David, The Wealth and Poverty of Nations, WW Norton, NY, 1999.

Lazonick, W., "What Happened To The Theory of Economic Development," in Higonnet, P., Landes, D., and Rosovsky, H., (editors), Favorites of Fortune, Harvard University Press, Cambridge, 1991.

Leontief, W., "Input-Output Data Base For Analysis of Technological Change," Economic Systems Research, 1, #3, 1989.

Linden, Greg , Dedrick, Jason and Kraemer, Kenneth L., "Innovation and Job Creation in a Global Economy: The Case of Apple's iPod," January 2009.

List, Frederick, The National System of Political Economy cited in Archibugi, Daniele, and Michie, Jonathan, Technology, Globalisation and Economic Performance, Cambridge University Press, Cambridge, 1997.

Los, B ., "The Empirical Performance of a New Interindustry Technology Spillover Measure", in: Nooteboom,B., and Saviotti,P., (eds), Technology and Knowledge: From the Firm to Innovation Systems, Edward Elgar, Cheltenham, UK, 2000.

Los, B . and Verspagen B., "R&D Spillovers and Productivity: Evidence from U .S. Manufacturing Microdata", Empirical Economics, vol. 25, 2000.

Los, B . and Verspagen, B., "Technology Spillovers and Their Impact on Productivity", in: Hanusch H., and Pyka, A., (eds), Companion to Neo-Schumpeterian Economics, Edward Elgar, Cheltenham, UK, 2007.

Macpherson, C. B. (Crawford Brough), The Political Theory of Possessive Individualism: Hobbes to Locke, Oxford, Clarendon Press, 1962.

Malerba, F. and L. Orsenigo, "Schumpeterian Patterns of Innovation," in Archibugi, D., and J. Michie, J., (eds.), Technology, Globalization and Economic Performance, Cambridge University Press, Cambridge, 1997.

Martin, Robert, Government by Dissent, NYU Press, N. Y. 2013.

McAdams, R., Paths of Fire: An Anthropologists Inquiry Into Western Technology, Princeton University Press, Princeton, NJ, 1996.

McDonald, Forrest, Novus Ordo Seclorum: The Intellectual Origins of the Constitution, Lawrence, Kan., University Press of Kansas, 1985.

McMath, Robert C., American Populism: A Social History, 1877 – 1898, Hill and Wang, NY, 1993.

McMath, Robert C., Populist Vanguard: A History of the Southern Farmers' Alliance, NewYork, Norton, 1975.

Merrill, Jensen, The Making of the American Constitution, D. Van Nostrand Co., Inc.,Princeton, N.J., 1964.

Meyers, Marvin, The Mind of the Founder: Sources of the Political Thought of James Madison, Hanover, N.H., Published for Brandeis University Press by University Press of New England, 1981.

Minsky, H. "Schumpeter: Finance and Evolution," in Heertje, A., and Perlman, M., (eds.), Evolving Technology and Market Structure: Studies in Schumpeterian Economics, University of Michigan Press, Ann Arbor, 1990.

Mokyr, J., The Lever of Riches: Technological Creativity and Economic Progress, Oxford University Press, New York, 1990.

Morroni, M., Production Processes and Technical Change, Cambridge University Press, Cambridge, 1992.

Mowery, D., (1998), Paths of Innovation: Technical Change in the 20th Century, Cambridge University Press, Cambridge, 1998.

Nelson, R. , "Technical Change As Cultural Evolution," in R. Thompson (ed.), Learning and Technical Change, St. Martin's Press, New York, 1993.

Onuf, Peter, Jeffersonian Legacies, 1993.

Pacheco, Josephine F., Antifederalism: The Legacy of George Mason (The George Mason Lecture Series) Hardcover – August, 1992.

Paine, Thomas, Common Sense (Dover Thrift Editions) unknown Edition by Thomas Paine

Palmer, Bruce, Man Over Money: The Southern Populist Critique of American Capitalism, UNC Press, CH, 1980.

Pasinetti, L., Structural Change and Economic Growth: A Theoretical Essay on The Dynamics of the Wealth of Nations, Cambridge University Press, Cambridge, 1981.

Peterson, Merrill D., The Jefferson Image in the American Mind, New York, Oxford University Press, 1960.

Poole, M., "Organizational Challenges In The New Forms," in G. DeSanctis and J. Fulk (eds.), Shaping Organizational Form: Communication, Connection and Community, Sage Public, Thousand Oaks, 1999.

Porat, M., The Information Economy: Definition and Measurement, Washington: U. S. Department of Commerce, 1977.

Porter, Michael E., et al., Problems Unsolved and a Nation Divided: The State of U.S. Competitiveness 2016, Including findings from Harvard Business School's 2016 surveys on U.S. competitiveness, Cambridge, MA, 2016.

Rakove, Jack N., Declaring Rights: A Brief History with Documents, Bedford Books. Boston, 1998.

Rawls, John, A Theory of Justice, Belknap Press of Harvard University Press, Cambridge, Mass.,1971.

Reiman, Jeffrey H., Justice and Modern Moral Philosophy, New Haven, Yale University Press, 1990.

Richardson, G. B.,"The Organization of Industry," Economic Journal, 82, 1972.

Rogers, E., "Diffusions of Innovations," cited in R. Goel (ed.), Economic Models of Technological Change:Theory and Application, Quorum Books, Westport, 1999.

Saviotti, P., Technological Evolution, Variety and the Economy, Edward-Elgar, Cheltenham, UK,1996.

Schacht, Wendy Cooperative R&D: Federal Efforts to Promote Industrial Competitiveness, CRS Report For Congress, Updated August 20, 2008.

Scott, Robert E., EPI Briefing Paper #147, November 17, 2003.

Siemers, David J., The Antifederalists: Men of Great Faith and Forbearance, Rowman & Littlefield. NY, 2003.

Sisson, Dan, The American Revolution of 1800: How Jefferson Rescued Democracy from Tyranny and Faction - and What This Means Today

Temin, P., "Entrepreneurs and Managers," in Higonnet, P., Landes, D., and Rosovsky, H.,(eds.), Favorites of Fortune, Harvard University Press, Cambridge, 1991 .

Thibaut, John W., and Kelley, John, The Social Psychology of Groups, New York, Wiley, 1959.

Vass, Laurie Thomas, Predicting Technology, 3rd Edition, Gabby Press, Raleigh, N. C., 2017.

Wigand, R., Picot, A., Reichwald, R., Information, Organization and Management, John Wiley & Sons, New York, 1997.

Williams, R., and Edge, D., "The Social Shaping of Technology," in Dutton, W., (ed.), Information and Communication Technologies: Visions and Realities, Oxford University Press, Oxford, 1996.

Wolff, E. "Spillovers, Linkages and Technical Change," Economic Systems Research, 9, #1, 1997.

Wood, Gordon S., The Creation of the American Republic, 1776 – 1787. WW Norton. NY, 1969.

Wood, Gordon S., The Radicalism of the American Revolution, Knopf. NY, 1992.

Utterback, James, Mastering the Dynamics of Innovation: How Companies Can Seize Opportunities In the Face of Technological Change, Harvard Business School Press, Boston, 1994.

Willenz, Sean , The Rise of American Democracy, W. W. Norton & Company, NY, 2006.

Wolf, Martin , Why Globalization Works, Yale University Press, New Haven, 2004.

Zuckert, Michael, The Natural Rights Republic: Studies In The Foundation of The American Political Tradition, University of Notre Dame Press, South Bend, 1996.

www.ingramcontent.com/pod-product-compliance
Lightning Source LLC
Chambersburg PA
CBHW072106040426
42334CB00042B/2495